Leonardo, Romancia and Ra

Michael Black

chipmunkapublishing
the mental health publisher

Published by
Chipmunkapublishing
PO Box 6872
Brentwood
Essex CM13 1ZT
United Kingdom

http://www.chipmunkapublishing.com

Chipmunkapublishing gratefully acknowledge the support of Arts Council England.

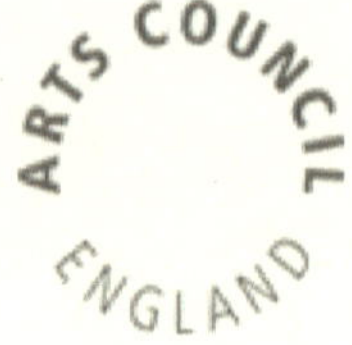

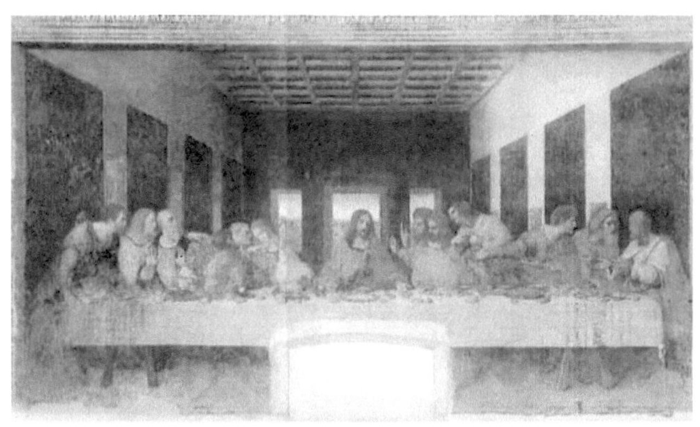

The Last Supper, Convent Of Sta. Maria delle Grazie, Milan, 1498, Leonardo da Vinci

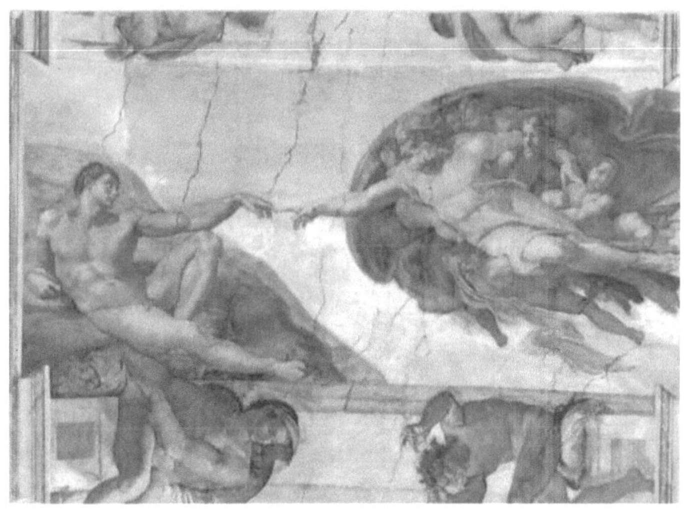

Creation Of Adam, Sistine Chapel Ceiling, The Vatican, Rome, 1508-1512, Michelangelo

Moderato

When I was younger I could sit in a room and knock off three songs a day, like 'Some Might Say' and 'Whatever' and a bunch of B-sides. But y'know, I'm not 26 any more. People think: Aw, give him two weeks and he'll write another album. It's not like that.
Noel Gallagher, *Oasis Talking*, p.114

The subtitle of *Stealing Heaven From God,* the unpublished book of which *Angels, Cleopatra And Psychosis* was an edited version, was *The Triumph Of The Artists*, and that is what this book is about. Traditionally, we learn that science was the triumph of the enlightenment, on Google there is even a site called "the triumph of science", but I radically disagree. The scientific revolution since approximately 1785, perhaps best summed up in Immanuel Kant's *The Critique Of Pure Reason*, actually offers false hope to us all and turns us all into analytic reductionists going nowhere. Whereas I am a romantic artist in the vein of Shelley and Géricault, I'm a Girondin by nature and thought, and I object. Angels exist, I've met four, but they'd never show up for a randomised angel existence control test! They object to the so-called triumph of science as much as I do!

Anyway, *Angels, Cleopatra And Psychosis* is what it is, and this book is the follow up. It uses the same technique of pulling out chapters from *Stealing Heaven From God* and making them work as stand alone short stories by contextualisation, but this time there are not five chapters, there are only three. And, please note, none are set on psychiatric wards. The experiences described in *Angels, Cleopatra And Psychosis* did not just occur on psychiatric wards, they were common to my life between 1993 and 2005 in general, and this book describes them. Yes, I end this book by saying that I have "uncover[ed] the mystery of God, the Sun God, and Creation", and yes, that's somewhat of a serious statement! But the visions and dreams I had during this period were by far the most important part of my life, and therefore I stand by the validity of their recollection. Further, particularly in terms of art history, they might be of interest to others.

I think romantics find their thirties very difficult. You are no longer young, but life hasn't begun at forty yet either, and your youthful charisma, which has always seen you through in the past, is fading. Your hair starts to thin! The waistline thickens! Whilst every one else is building stable and sensible lives, you're still dreaming of revelation and revolution, of reinventing the world anew! Géricault died in his thirties after all, and I think I was lucky to survive mine. Shelley died aged twenty nine. Noel Gallagher (the song writer of *Oasis*) used to say that in his twenties he felt guilty if he didn't write a song a day, but now in his forties he's lucky if he writes one a month, and to reach that point of self-realisation, he's a lucky man as well. I feel much the same. I don't fill up notebooks in the way I did fifteen years ago, I'm not "chasing the fade" any more. I've finally grown up, but it's been a wild ride!

Anyway, if *Angels, Cleopatra And Psychosis* was my rock'n'roll album, this book is my literary sonata, hat tipped to Ludwig van Beethoven *et al,* the master of the [piano] sonata form. It's not entirely consistent with the earlier book, but then spirits and angels are no more entirely consistent than people are. Or Sun Gods. But you'll meet three new spirits along the way, so happy reading and hope you like it!

Michael Black, Macclesfield, July 2009

A Lesson from Leonardo

The same end terraced house in north York, late Spring 1994, just after Devil At The Door (see Angels, Cleopatra And Psychosis). I rebuilt my computer, and continued to work on my experimental novel Crossing Out The Emperor. The spirits of Leonardo da Vinci and Michelangelo were simply around every day, and I got used to their presence as one gets used to the silent presence of a partner, or a dog or a cat. But their personalities were radically different. Leonardo was stable and assured, Michelangelo on the other hand was all over the place, up one day, down the next. When he was down he lay on the floor in depression, and when he was up he literally floated on the ceiling. Our conversations were wide ranging, of which this is an example, but of one thing Leonardo and Michelangelo were both convinced. God wanted the world to end in the year 2000.

"I think", I said, "that it is about time I was let in on considerably more information. After all, this is my house, we are surrounded by little red devils, and you are both living in it. So, cards on the table please!"

"That's fair enough", said Leonardo. "But let's be practical about this. Generally speaking Michael, it isn't worth looking into what happened before you were born. The objective facts at the time you are born will always be your first reality"

"That's fine", I said, "but it doesn't take me very far"

"It's not really supposed to. But it is a very good way to remain sane. In fact, it's the foundation of the way most people think, and most people are sane Michael, even if they are also incurious and frequently gullible. Understanding the reality surrounding you at birth stops all kinds of unnecessary speculations Michael. For example, is the universe expanding or contracting? Will it all end in three or four billion years time? Who cares? It is simply too long to contemplate, and it's also complete hogwash when God wants the whole planet to vanish down a black hole in approximately six years time anyway. Believe NASA and you will believe anyone!"

"I'm still not convinced about God's intentions", I said. "I mean how? Planets can't simply vanish!"

"How do you know Michael? And believe me, I do know exactly what I am talking about. There's five hundred years work behind this. It's pre-programmed Michael and I am positive. The issue is simple. God is bored by his own Creation, and would much rather shut the whole planet down rather than let his ultimate slaves, that is human beings, that is the only animals on the planet conscious of His existence, try and run it in more creative ways than he has ever imagined, and that, ultimately, means the planet should be run by artists. I have a wide definition when it comes to artists Michael, I mean engineers and architects as well as poets and painters – or playwrights – but I do mean artists. Who struggles to inspire people Michael, or make the world a more beautiful place? It certainly isn't politicians, or psychiatrists for that matter. It is artists. So, obviously, all good artists are at war with God Michael, and they always have been".

"But you painted *The Last Supper*!" I said. "How can you be at war with God when you create a painting like that!?"

"Michael, that is very well said, and that fresco, to be precise, is the ultimate proof of my real intentions".

"You're going to like this story Michael!", said Michelangelo, laughing again from the ceiling.

"Put succinctly Michael, in modern parlance so to speak, *The Last Supper* is a piss take. But before we talk about it, let us talk about history. In fact, why don't you talk about history Michael. After all, *Crossing Out The Emperor*, as you are well aware, is trying to break out of history, isn't it, and not so much recreate the past as make it breathe again as living fragments of meaningful time".

I couldn't believe how well Leonardo expressed himself, but I simply agreed.

"History has always fascinated me", I said, "although even at my grammar school it was appallingly badly taught in the main. Notes from the blackboard and very seldom any more. But it is bringing history to life that has always fired me", I continued. "That's why my main literary heroes are Sir Walter Scott and Alexandre Dumas *pére*. It's no coincidence that in *Waverley*, the first historical novel, Scott, who invented the form after all, basically leaves out the bloody and disgusting slaughter of the battlefield of Culloden Moor and prefers to concentrate on a saner and more romantic future which, admittedly, but not surprisingly, he has some difficulty creating. In fact, you could say that historical novelists are at war with academic historians. Academic historians want to pin history down with facts and records as proofs of "what really happened", whereas historical novelists – and they are a popular force of their own including Catherine Cookson and Jean Plaidy amongst them – want to challenge the historical record, they want to make it more exciting, more romantic and more energetic. Historical novelists are energetic by their nature, and like Scott and Dumas build their own antiquitous homes at Abbotsford and the Château de Monte-Cristo for example, as well as writing reams and reams that challenge the received historical record, whereas I have never met an energetic academic historian in my life, and I've met a few. It was even a problem at Cambridge! What has always fascinated me is not history, it is the relationship between history and literature, so in fact at Cambridge I ended up writing a historical thesis in the English department. Even now I'm not sure how I got away with it".

"Very well said, Michael", said Michelangelo

"So continue", said Leonardo

"Continue with what?", I said. "I've finished".

"No you haven't", said Leonardo. "Say whatever comes into your head next".

So I did.

"As Gustav Flaubert (the author of *Madame Bovary*) once put it, "always research the subject thoroughly, but always have the guts to ignore the evidence when it suits you"".

"Precisely!", said Leonardo, "and in this case, ultimately, ignoring the evidence means ignoring the fact that God wants to end the world".

"History is a grudge", I said. "Established history is always the record of the winners, of the powerful, and most academic historians might as well be monks so far as I can see, as well as belonging intrinsically to one establishment or another. The powerful always claim to have God on their side, so History becomes the record of God. Get rid of God and you get rid of History itself! And that strikes me as a wonderful idea, and not far off how I approached *Crossing Out The Emperor*! I don't want complete histories of anything! I want pertinent recorded instances of lives before our own that still resonate with meanings, and that is something different entirely! Further, historical novelists – unlike academic historians – sometimes make the facts up, to their credit, simply because there has to be a better story than the one God, if God creates History, forces us to live in. And what is a fact that can be ascertained anyway, and ascertained by whom? An academic historian with permission to the right libraries full of the official government records, or a historical novelist probably without access to most of them. What is an historical fact, and why record it? That is the issue of the warfare, one of the greatest issues of civilisation itself. Is the most important fact about 1812 Napoleon's march on Russia, or is it Beethoven falling in love, as I believe he did, with Antonie Brentano that year? And which event has the most promise to it?"

I was by now simply flying, saying things in the right way that I had always wanted to say but always struggled to, and I had almost entirely forgotten the nature of the exulted company I was still keeping. Leonardo and Michelangelo were simply becoming my friends.

"Gentlemen", I concluded, "I have an idea. If you two are such wise old friends, then might I request admittance to your company. We could become a new version of *The Three Musketeers* themselves!"

"Except", said Leonardo, "in that case there were of course four, if d'Artagnan is included, and as you are well aware, that has it's own kind of magic. The Three Musketeers always add up to more than the sum of their parts. You have almost said it all about history Michael, and I shall now say the rest for you – being considerably older than you I have after all witnessed far more history than you have – and I shall start with *The Last Supper* itself, saying in advance, that if you think academic historians are a tiresome breed of monks, then you should meet art historians and painting restorers. They are even worse! There are art historians the world over Michael who will tell you that *The Last Supper* is a triumph of form and content, but as far as I am concerned it is far too narrow and far too long, rather like history itself. And of course, since Michelangelo and I represent the two greatest flowerings of Renaissance Man, Michael, we did see a few things coming even in around 1500. Firstly we could see even then that the Day of Judgement and Armageddon in the year 2000 was clearly going to be true.

It was obvious even then that the 20th century was going to be a nightmare, if only because of the advances in military technology based on metal and high explosives that were beginning to be made even then. I even designed some prototypes myself after all, my submarine for example. We could both see Panzer tanks and bombs from the sky coming, so to speak, although obviously, Hiroshima and Nagasaki took even us by surprise until we started to think about it. But it was obvious that the 20th century would be the century of total war, and it was also obvious that advances in medical science combined with the European powers nascent interest in Empire would ultimately lead to a very overcrowded planet. Six billion people on planet Earth Michael!"

"Nine billion by 2050 according to UN figures", I interjected

"That is totally unsustainable, and beyond a certain point, advances in medical science are a very mixed blessing anyway. Medicated survival is not life…"

"Yes, yes", I said, somewhat impatiently. "I agree. But I still want to know why *The Last Supper* is a piss take, and if we are all in this together, I want to be totally convinced".

"Very well then", said Leonardo. "Oh, the impatience of youth Michelangelo!"

"Isn't it wonderful!", said the voice on the ceiling.

"To *The Last Supper* then. Apart from the fact that it is too narrow and too long, Michael, the biggest single thing about *The Last Supper* is that I painted it on a damp monastery wall. In other words, I wanted it to fall off the wall as soon as possible, and I only did it for the money, which, being a living, breathing mortal at the time I badly needed. So, you can understand my frustration with art historians and painting restorers can't you when, five hundred years later, *The Last Supper* is still on the walls, constantly patched up again. And of course, it has now been patched up so many times in so many places that there can't be a single brush stroke left that was ever mine anyway! So how is it that my name is still associated with it? Apparently, I am still the genius responsible for it!"

"Which, in a way, he is Michael", said Michelangelo, "but he doesn't like the word *genius*, and neither do I…"

"Neither do I", I said

"And neither do you, and Leonardo is only a genius in respect of *The Last Supper* Michael, in as much as it declares war on Christianity, and God, and history, all at the same time".

"The Last Supper, Michael", said Leonardo. "What an awful title! How depressing! No more food, no more life after this one guys! Get rid of History and you get rid of God Michael, you said it yourself, and from your young perspective at the end of the 20th century you are correct, but from my perspective in approximately 1500, I thought, and I still think, it is actually the other way around. Get rid of God, and you get rid of History. Great artists have never been truly religious Michael. They simply had Christianity forced upon them with endless forced commissions to paint churches and cathedrals and so on. And Michelangelo and I are no exceptions. So there I was, forced to paint *The Last Supper*, with all kinds of questions in my mind that I could not possibly paint into reality. History makes you think backwards Michael, which is why it is called *The Last Supper*. Why isn't it called *The First Supper*? Even if it was the last meal of Jesus, the title would still be apt in terms of establishing a new religion! But that is not what God had in mind. History makes people think backwards because it locks them into a closed down time sequences of 2000 years with no way out".

"That's why historical novelists are forced to invent history!", I suddenly found myself saying. "It's the only way to generate enough energy and life to survive past the end of time! And life in a closed down time sequence of course makes successful romance and happy endings…"

"How about happy *beginnings*?, Michael", said Leonardo.

"Exactly!, I said. "Life in a closed down time sequence makes successful romance and happy beginnings totally impossible, which is why historical novelists all insist on romance as essential. They don't write about the past, they heroically demand the possibility of a future!"

"Quite so. Meanwhile, whilst God continues to run History, or the other way around, the real possibilities of new adventures and new ideas and new sanities decrease as there are more and more people on the planet and travel becomes more commonplace and faster, making real space and time effectively shrink. And then there is the question of women Michael".

"The Last Supper you mean?"

"Yes"

"I've always wondered about that one myself", I said.

"Well, it is an obvious question isn't it. *Why, why, why* are there no recorded histories – to use a word we all now know we dislike – of female apostles? *Why?* There *must* have been female apostles Michael, because without women it is obvious that any new religious movement – or any other kind of movement – has no future. And if you knew you were going to be crucified Michael, would you have supper surrounded only by men? I certainly wouldn't!"

"Neither would I!", said Michelangelo. "I'd definitely want some women around, and a few loose ones too".

"Suitably irreverent, and very well said", said Leonardo. "For once on the matter of women Michael, Michelangelo and myself agree, although it is usually an argument".

"Why?", I said.

"Basically", said Michelangelo, "Leonardo as a spirit does not and never has missed physical sex, whereas I most definitely always have done, and what's more, still do. What shall we reveal next Leonardo? The true meanings of evolution, or the story of the Sistine Chapel Ceiling?"

"This is fantastic!", I said. "Real education at last!"

"Honoured to of service", said Leonardo, "and it is a privilege to have such an attentive listener".

At this point, Michelangelo took over.

"The Sistine Chapel Ceiling Michael, is in many ways the opposite of the *The Last Supper*. For a start, that one was seriously well plastered, and it is definitely not falling off the Vatican ceiling. In fact, I hope it stays there forever, and they can keep it as far as I'm concerned, and no, Michael, I definitely did not want to paint it. In fact, when I was approached, I tried to get Raphael to do it, and only Leonardo – and we didn't get on at the time – persuaded me otherwise. He told me I had no choice, and he convinced me he was right".

"Why didn't you get on?", I asked

"Stupid professional jealousies Michael", interjected Leonardo, "of the common sort. I was older than him, I thought Michelangelo an upstart, he thought me conservative. And we were both right. But the real story of the Sistine Chapel ceiling sorted out the disagreements Michael…"

"… And we are both extremely proud to inform you", said Michelangelo, "that you won't find this one in anyone's history books at all. The story is ours and ours alone".

How could I be more intrigued than I already was? But I was! I liked having these guys around. I lit a cigarette.

"You smoke too much Michael", said Leonardo, "but it doesn't matter for now. And besides, we are almost certain to need some flames at some point, and a lighter will definitely do. But make sure you buy some spares in for when the invisible Cardinal comes back. The rest is always about timing".

"Tell me more", I said.

"Firstly, as you know, Michelangelo did not want to do the Sistine Chapel ceiling at all".

"Why?"

"Because", said Michelangelo, "it was too big and too vast, and it had all kinds of problems of visual perspective that I hadn't solved at the time and didn't really want to. And it was obvious to me that it would mean years spent lying on my back on scaffolding getting paint in my eyes. So, no thank you".

"And then there is the problem of the religiousness Michael", added Leonardo. "Real artists never like painting churches, and by that standpoint, painting the chapel of the Pope is tantamount to slavery. I might paint *The Last Supper* for my own ultimate purposes, but the Sistine Chapel is something else entirely…"

"… but until Leonardo pointed all this out to me Michael, I'd never really thought about these issues in my life", continued Michelangelo. "I'd just assumed artists always worked on religious themes for the simple reason we all had to. So I didn't want to do it anyway, and then Leonardo said "you've got to do it", and then I said "I'm not doing it, and I've told the Vatican to try Raphael". And then Leonardo said "that's even worse than you doing it, mate!", and I said "why?", and then Leonardo said "because he's a better painter than you are", and that one really annoyed me..."

"I can imagine", I said. I had started to laugh.

"... but I was finally forced to admit it was true. We almost had a fist fight Michael! As in "you're past it Leonardo", "OK, then, come on Michelangelo, try me!"

"Raphael had no equals as a painter Michael", said Leonardo. "And even today, even the finest painting forgers will never try a Raphael, which to me is the ultimate compliment"

"I couldn't name a single Raphael if I tried", I was forced to admit.

"Doesn't matter. Believe me. Fantastic, but no real brain"

"And he couldn't sculpt Michael", said Michelangelo, "which I definitely could do"

"I am aware of that. Your *David*"

"Enough said"

"Anyway", resumed Leonardo. "I pointed out to Michelangelo that if he didn't like the Vatican, and I most certainly didn't like them either, then what was the profit of giving them the best painter imaginable to paint their most hallowed ceiling?"

"So it's another piss take?"

"It's a bit more than that Michael, but you're on the right lines". Michelangelo was laughing too.

"Raphael would have been a complete disaster Michael", said Leonardo. "Being such a good painter, he would have painted the whole thing blue I reckon, because good painters always love blue, the colour of the sky on a good day itself, when light – and what else do any painters ever paint? - is able to fully declare itself.

Think of Fra Angelica, think of Kandinsky, think of Picasso's blue period, there are thousands of examples".

"So basically Michael, I agreed to paint the Sistine Chapel, and to make sure that the ceiling colour was predominantly grey".

"Grey? Is that all there is to it?"

"Far from it", said Leonardo, "but it was a very good place to start".

"And now, in 1994", said Michelangelo, somewhat triumphantly, "apparently we have a Pope – and I have nothing against him personally – who is so crippled he can't even raise his head up to look at his own grey interior sky, so to speak".

"The one thing they weren't getting from us Michael, was a blue sky. No sunny days inside the Vatican, thank you very much. And then the real rows started!"

"The *Creation of Adam*, Michael", said Michelangelo.

"And it was my idea to demand it", said Leonardo, "or rather demand it through Michelangelo. Oh, and by the way, we almost painted it together. I dressed up half the time as the palette mixer looking stupid and always getting ignored. No one knew it was me at all!"

"You've lost me", I said, still laughing.

"Oh, there were praying cardinals all over the place Michael", said Leonardo. "And there's me mixing up the Dulux, so to speak! But back to the *Creation of Adam*. This is all about killing God before he kills the planet, all about questioning Paradise, and all about evolution in the end, which I had by no means worked out Michael, but I had started to think about it. I mean it is obvious that reptiles must be descended from amphibians, and it has been obvious for thousands of years that monkeys resemble human beings in many respects. But that can wait".

"What matters is that as the painter", said Michelangelo, "when the Vatican said, "the *Creation of Adam*, please", I said, "if God created Man in His image, then I must paint God in human form". And they didn't like it one bit Michael, because to them, God was something so Divine he could hardly be painted at all. God – so to speak – knows what else they wanted, but they certainly didn't like what I said next either. Because I said, "God must be pretty old by now you know, so at the very least, he must be going bald!" Sacrilege! The cardinals weren't having that one, so I said "OK, he's going grey then""'

"Just like the sky Michael. In other words, Michelangelo painted a God who is clearing getting old, that is, ultimately dying Michael, which is a big victory. And the Vatican can't deny it, because whether they like this version of events or not, the proof is on their own ceiling to this day. And "don't worry", I said to Michelangelo, "we'll make Him bald next time". If God dies History dies Michael. Winning at last! Which brings me to God's biggest problem in my opinion Michael, namely that I don't think in His greatness – the Big Bang, the Creation of the Universe, the Beginning of Time or whatever – he ever thought about dying at all, and dying for everyone, spirit or otherwise is a good idea in the end. Everyone fulfils their destiny and has no other purpose eventually, only in God's case He won't accept this, and he'd much rather Planet Earth died than he did".

"And we decided to disagree with Him, Michael", said Michelangelo, "simple as that"

"I'm not surprised", I said, "now you put it like that. I happen to disagree myself!"

"We thought you might"

"*The Last Supper* instead of *The First Supper* Michael, said Leonardo, it goes on and on. God is a bastard and no mistake. It is as simple as that. Look at that film *The Greatest Story Ever Told* about Christ's crucifixion when John Wayne says at the end "truly this man was the Son of God". How the hell does he know? The only person walking around Palestine calling himself the Son of God was Christ himself and that is bound to make a lot of other people rather angry. I'm sure Christ believed it, simply because it was God's voice telling him to! Have you had a risen Christ delusion yet Michael?"

"Yes I have", I said. "Michelangelo said it was a trick of the invisible Cardinal"

"Well it probably was. But I'm sure you'll have some more, directly from God Himself. It will doubtless be terrifying, but you'll survive them"

"What, God's voice inside my head telling me I am Christ reborn?"

"Exactly that Michael, and I can't wait. That way I can measure the strength of God's imagination Michael, and we are both convinced yours is stronger, so there"

"Wow!", I said. "My imagination is more powerful than God's? What does that mean? That God is weak, or I am strong?"

"Both of course. And don't worry. You are mortal. Flesh and bone. Nothing more or less, so there"

"Well, God can try and convince me of whatever he likes, but I don't want to be Christ anyway. I'm Michael Black and I like it that way. And I sure as hell don't want to be crucified!"

"Exactly. Which is the point at which Christ Himself realised God was a bastard too. "My God, why hasth thou forsaken me". Simply because God is nasty and spiteful. It is obvious Michael, and it has always been obvious. Except the Vatican constantly want to confuse the meaning by making it mystical and beyond the comprehension of ordinary mortals, which it clearly isn't"

"That must be why I sang the Bob Dylan lyric in Newark police station"

"Of course it is Michael", said Michelangelo. "You knew it all along, and I couldn't believe you sang that one myself! And with real venom and perfect pitch if I might say so"

"I go on and on when I get onto the subject of God Michael", said Leonardo.

"He does indeed!"

"I mean, if God wanted Jesus to succeed, then why didn't He tell Him that the world was round?! Why not? Think of the impact that would have caused! No one anywhere had thought of that one 2000 years ago! And it is the kind of piece of crucial information a father would tell a sacred son, isn't it?! And God must have known, because he created the planet after all! Not to mention all the other ones as well. Because if there is only one God now Michael, then there has always been one God, which means Zeus is the same guy using a different name, and he was crazy too and so forth and so on. *The Greatest Story Ever Told.* History forcing everyone to think backwards once again. If Christ's crucifixion is the greatest story ever told, then we all have no chance! What about *The Greatest Story Ever Told... So Far, And Who's Got A Better One Because It Can't Be That Hard*!"

"What about making God go bald?", I said, laughing to myself at this glorious blasphemy.

"Oh, well, the Victorians did that on their own Michael, at the height of the British Empire when of course, and you said it yourself, they must have been convinced they had God on their side as well. After Michelangelo had painted God as a greying man on the Sistine Chapel ceiling, the Victorians started to depict God as an old bald man sitting on a cloud. I couldn't believe that one myself. Bingo! I mean if that is all the energy God possesses as some kind of super-being, then it isn't very impressive is it? And then, and then, Michael…"

"You'll love this one kid", said Michelangelo

"…we finally get evolution revealed to us all by none other than Charles Darwin, a Victorian too! And who does he look like Michael? Come on, who?"

"God", I said. It was all suddenly obvious.

"So just as some people in the western world at least had finally started to seriously doubt God's very existence, Charles Darwin shows up and says "I agree, it's all down to evolution". God in disguise Michael, congratulating Himself, so to speak, on revealing his own secrets that he's known all along but has never told anyone else. I mean people have been speculating about the origins of life forever Michael, but no one knew remotely where to look for the evidence, and then Darwin comes along, sails aboard the *HMS Beagle* and cracks the whole subject in about four years! Impossible! The Galapagos Islands and so forth Michael! How come Darwin knew all the right places on the planet to go to? Strange to put it mildly. And I had some spiritual rows with Charles Darwin about this Michael, believe me, and that was definitely God alright! The power source inside

His brain! Unbelievable! But not so strong as when He first met me, because I told him straight. "I don't believe for a moment you are really Charles Darwin, you are God in disguise, and I'm coming after you, and what's more so is Michelangelo", and He got the message Michael. And guess what! In his old age, he tried re-reading Shakespeare and said he didn't like it. Of course not! Jealous of the talents of His human slave when they rebel Michael, just as always. And all artistic creation is always a rebellion against God, simple as that"

"The most important book I've ever read is Albert Camus' *The Rebel*", I said.

"I know that Michael. I've watched you over the years as well. Need I say more? Before you rebel against the constrictions that surround you, you never do anything. The important thing is to rebel in a positive way. Evolution Michael! God's ultimate game! Who on earth allows a creature like Tyrannosaurus Rex to stalk the planet? That's not an active carnivore, that's a raging maniac, for the simple reason its arms are too tiny to ever reach its mouth. It can't even feed itself properly. Imagine the frustration of that! Deformed as a species and bound to end up insane and tearing flesh off anything that moves whether hungry or not!"

"I'm very hungry", I said, "and I need a bacon sandwich"

"Very well", said Leonardo. "I think that is quite enough for one day"

Adagio

Well now. There's a fragment if ever there was one, but one typical of the kind of conversation Leonardo, Michelangelo and I had during those spring days of 1994 in York.

And suffice to say (unless I am much mistaken!), that the planet didn't vanish in the year 2000 after all, but then that's only because you've got Leonardo and Michelangelo to thank for it. They made sure it didn't, in a head to head argument with God Himself, and it's a very long story. Essentially, God wanted to die and take the planet with Him, and Leonardo and Michelangelo managed to keep Him alive. God survived, and so did the planet. Just.

And so did John Black. Strange! When my father had his stroke in 1982, the doctors gave him two or three years maximum, and yet he was to live for another twenty three! Oh for a plastic heart valve and a pacemaker! Oh, for the triumph of science itself!

To an artist, whether the earth moves round the sun or vice-versa is a matter of supreme indifference, whereas to a scientist of course it is crucial. So long as the sun comes up in the morning, I don't care about the reasons why, whereas a scientist does. And scientists rule the world, not artists, which is why arts budgets are so tiny next to those the scientific community can get their hands on. Except it's not that simple. Ultimately, you can't *prove* what is good art or bad art except by long established consensus, but then can you ever *prove* what is good science? Will we still believe in Einstein in fifty years time? Many scientific discoveries have actually (although this is seldom pointed out) discredited previous science in the process, and yet our faith in science apparently still grows!

This is particularly true of medical science, and for the Hippocratic oath, simply read "most people are cowards and afraid of dying" in my opinion. In that sense, the NHS has been a disaster, because medical science can now technically keep virtually anyone alive almost indefinitely. And at *vast* expense! However, whilst you can't deny the technical skill behind an open-heart operation, you can question the technical and diagnostic skills of the average psychiatrist, psychiatry being a false science that has somehow piggybacked its way to respectability using the triumph of science as its disguise. The average psychiatrist is simply a medic who has done a psychiatry conversion course at the end of their degree, and it sucks. *Modern psychiatry does not make sense*, and physical and mental ailments are two entirely different things that should never have been confused in the first place. In other words, the medical profession have no right to own the subject of madness at all, and in essence, they don't know what they are talking about. *Modern psychiatry exists only to zombify the apparently abnormal, and act as the ultimate agent of social control.* As Thomas Szasz once put it, "deviant behaviour is freedom of choice", but psychiatrists don't see it that way. Psychiatrists are the key holders of mental hospitals, and mental hospitals exist in so-called democracies to ensure that conviction without trial still exists via the backdoor. Psychiatrists are the thought police.

Further, the average psychiatrist has no interest or empathy with the so-called "psychotic" or spiritual experiences of the patient, and simply uses drugs to obliterate them, whether the patient becomes a zombie in the process or otherwise. Rocket science modern psychiatry is not, it's a scientific joke. But it's also a joke with a vast financial turnover, and the NHS psychiatric drugs bill must be vast as well.

I'd reached this point in my thinking by about 1998, which is also the time I moved out of my mother's house to live on my own in Macclesfield. And it's also the time when Dr. Chung my GP wrote to my psychiatrist questioning the diagnosis of schizophrenia (so I've not only had four mental health diagnoses, the medical profession has also said there's nothing wrong with me as well!). And as I recount in *Angels, Cleopatra And Psychosis* I was on Clozaril from 1995 to 2001, which I describe as a "dream to be on". This needs qualifying. It was only a dream to be on relative to being on Clopixol previously! I'd still much rather have been on nothing at all!

On Clozaril I was stable, and I had minimum contact with the mental health world from 1995 to 2001. I even managed to return to writing in 1998 (I am a writer through and through, but I actually met a psychiatrist in York who told my mother that writing had "damaged me"!), but of spirit worlds I knew nothing, and had no contact with Leonardo and Michelangelo between 1994 and 2001 at all. I deduce from this that Clozaril obliterated my spiritual receptivity, and it was only when the dose was reduced around the year 2000 that at least some of my spiritual receptivity returned and I met Leonardo and Michelangelo again during the summer of 2001.

I met them again when I was on Adelphi ward. You might say that this proves I only met the delusion of them because I'd gone mad again, but I radically disagree. That summer I was diagnosed as clinically high, and I had a great time relaxing in the Adelphi ward courtyard in the summer sun, but that's it. Psychotic I was not. And I would argue I wasn't clinically high at all, I was just artistically inspired. "Is it mental illness or is it artistic inspiration?", I once said to Dr. J.S. Bowie, to which he replied "I will decide". But then he was the scientist and I was the artist. Excuse me, Dr. Bowie, but I am the one who will decide! I know far more about these things than you do! There were good reasons for me to be high in the summer of 2001 after all. I'd started thinking about my Dora Maar play, I'd started to think about what would become *Stealing Heaven From God.* I was filling up notebooks one after the other. Life in many ways was good!

By this time my father's partner Peggy had tried to kill herself, and John Black (aka God) was just a drunk Barclay Park Nursing home, getting paralytic whenever he could on scotch, still dreaming of his own oblivion and that of the planet. Leonardo and Michelangelo told me all about their battles with Him to stop the planet vanishing the previous year, and I had many battles with my father's own imagination in my dreams that summer as well. He would try to make the planet vanish down a big black hole, I would always resist the gravitational pull and stop it happening at the last moment. It was Him or me, it was as simple as that.

Anyway, Leonardo, Michelangelo and me, the Two Musketeers and their apprentice, prevailed. The planet was saved, and saved by artists at that, so I pronounce this to be an artists' planet! The triumph of science was a false dawn, and a new age is upon us where the triumph of art will prevail!

Meanwhile, when I was on Adelphi ward in 2001, something else happened of great beauty and significance. Romancia, Leonardo da Vinci's girlfriend, escaped from five hundred years trapped in Hell. She suddenly appeared coming up through the floor of the smoking lounge at 3am, a vision of female beauty and fecundity personified. She was free at last, having been cast into Hell's lowest sulphurous depths upon her death so long ago, and gradually, against great opposition, she had climbed all the stairs to her final escape.

Leonardo spent most of the summer trying to keep John Black's imagination stable at Barclay Park, so he wasn't there to witness the event. But I was. I welcomed Romancia as Leonardo's beloved with open arms. I was her protector as I was Leonardo's friend. Romancia announced it remained her intention to become "the wind of love", and was almost ready to vanish on the summer breeze immediately. But I persuaded her she needed time to recuperate first. Put bluntly, it was clear that after five hundred years in Hell, Romancia needed a break.

In *Angels, Cleopatra And Psychosis*, I mention going to Paris in the summer of 2001 and state "but that's another story". Here it is. I took Romancia on holiday.

Romancia in Paris

I have visions like no other
So romantic you'll discover
Humdrum, *The Corrs*

I arrived on Adelphi ward in the summer of 2001 for one simple reason. I had an argument with my mother at her house, walked out, and she rang for the police! The police lifted me half way up the road and took me straight to Adelphi ward, driving far too fast as they did so I might add (yes all this strikes me a legally dubious in the extreme as well, but there we are!). There was absolutely nothing mentally wrong with me as far as I was concerned, but after my experiences of the Parkside asylum six years previously, Adelphi ward certainly took me by surprise! Single bedrooms? Smoking lounges and shower rooms? Well, it was better than working at Stockport MBC with all its political infighting, that was for sure! For some reason I was immediately put on a Section 3, for "up to six months", but I decided not to worry about it, and enjoy courtyard life in the summer sun instead. And the only drug they put me on was Clozaril, which I was on already, so it made no difference to me. In short, I was already treating psychiatric wards like free hotels. When Romancia escaped from Hell, I had been on Adelphi ward for about a month, and Dr. Bowie was on the verge of releasing me from the Section 3, but wanted me to spend a week at home first. I said I'd rather go to Paris. He said "that's OK". I cleared the idea with Michelangelo as well, who told me I would meet two new spirits in Paris I had long admired who would help me protect Romancia. I took Romancia to Paris on tenterhooks...

Why had I booked a double room with Romancia? On the reflection of walking back from the travel agent, I wasn't so sure it was a good idea. How would Romancia feel about sleeping in the same bed with me alone? Two single rooms would have been out of the question (I could hardly have kept a single room free for a spirit other people apparently could not see), but I could have tried to book a twin room after all.

However, when I discussed the situation with Romancia back on Adelphi ward she didn't mind. Romancia accepted my honest assessment of my own actions, namely that I'd done what I'd done because I felt that a double room and us both sleeping in the same double bed was the easiest and most reliable way of making sure she was safe. That way I'd know immediately if there was any trouble with cardinals, devils or the like. Romancia was obviously reassured by this and simply laughed. "A holiday", she said, "at last".

But here the problems started. Romancia adapted to the limited life of Adelphi ward quite quickly, and after Hell of course it appeared like Paradise to her. She loved sitting in the sun of the courtyard, and also spent along time sleeping during the days in my bed, but of modernity she knew nothing. The television, which I advised her to mistrust absolutely, frightened her, and cathode ray tubes, moving pictures *et al* seemed too much to explain for now. So I didn't, or at least not immediately.

"Everything will need explaining to me", said Romancia. "I have been in Hell for five hundred years, and Hell is death. You are given no knowledge of the future. That's what death is. Darkness and ignorance. To me transport is a horse, and it hasn't even been proven beyond dispute the world is round yet, though Leonardo had his suspicions. So what on earth are those moving carriages with no horses outside the windows?"

They were of course cars, which looked like magic to Romancia, but in simple terms I put her right about that one.

"There is something that has been invented called an internal combustion engine", I said. "Cars are all over the place, in fact there are far too many of them. An engine works on oil, and you extract oil from the ground. Oil is basically decayed trees from millions of years ago"
"So there aren't many horses around any more?"
"Very few"
"So we will go to Paris in a car and take a boat as well?", asked Romancia.

And here was my biggest problem. How could I explain jet technologies that now allowed aeroplanes to fly at 30,000 feet at 600 miles an hour that would take us to Paris instead? And that once we had got to Manchester airport, the whole journey would take less than two hours. Romancia was imagining a journey taking days. She was also imagining a chance to see something of England and France, whereas in fact of course we would see very little but sky.

"You can't be telling me the truth!", said Romancia. "There are now metal flying machines that will transport us to Paris in two hours?"

"Less than"

"Well that's a miracle to me. Does Leonardo know?"

"Of course he knows. And he probably understands all the technologies involved a great deal better than I do. And Michelangelo knows too by the way. We now live in a very technological world Romancia"

"Michelangelo knows? So they are still together?"

"Yes. I've actually lived with both of them. Leonardo is stable and wise, Michelangelo was all over the place for a long time, but he's getting better now. The Sistine Chapel ceiling wrecked his head for centuries. Too many readings of the Old Testament prophets I should imagine. Too many prophets wreck your head"

"And we shall fly how high?"

"About 30,000 feet in the air Romancia. Above the clouds"

"That's high enough to meet God", said Romancia.

"No it isn't. Believe me. I've done it before. You just look down on clouds, that's all. If there ever was a Heaven above the clouds, it would appear to have vanished. And that's our whole point really. Leonardo, Michelangelo and I, Romancia, are involved in a very big argument with God, who would appear to have dropped down to earth due to decrepit old age. But it's a long story"

Romancia asked no more questions at this point, and, essentially, off to Paris we went that 16th day of

July 2001 in the evening after I'd returned from Culcheth, near Warrington, England, having cleared out the remainder of my possessions from my father's house, including the cooker. Airports were new to Romancia as well of course, and she couldn't believe the size of the plane we were getting on. But we were at the airport long enough for her to be reassured by seeing planes both take off and land.

"So it's really true she said. Metal birds that can fly"

The flight, after the exhilarating acceleration of the take off to her, was disappointing. In the late evening, we didn't even see the sky in any clarity, and of course in a pressurised cabin you get no sensation of altitude or of the thinness of the atmosphere at the height you are travelling. Romancia sat on my knee throughout the flight, and it passed off uneventfully.

As for me, I was more concerned with getting to the hotel once we arrived at Charles de Gaulle airport, but arriving there made me realise how much history of five hundred years I was going to have to try and explain, and how difficult it was going to be.

"Who is Charles de Gaulle?", asked Romancia.
"An ex-President of France", I said.
"A President? And what is that?"
"He's the elected ruler"
"You mean there isn't a king any more?"
"No. The revolution saw to that"
"The revolution! And what was that?"

But then I felt up to the challenge of all this. If I couldn't explain French revolutionary history to Romancia with ten days in Paris to do it, then I couldn't explain anything at all, and I was sure I could.

At the same time, as we left Charles de Gaulle airport and got on the bus to Opéra, I was wondering who were the two spiritual protectors we were to met in Paris that Michelangelo had referred to before I left England. My only concern that evening was getting myself and Romancia to the hotel as fast as possible, but I wondered if we would be met by the same two august spirits at Opéra itself.

Romancia however was awestruck by the lights of the highway as we drove into Paris. Arriving at Opéra in all its majesty, no spirits met us, and I immediately hailed a taxi to the hotel. By the time we got there it was past midnight. Luckily however, the hotel had an *Alimentation* right next to it that was still open, and I bought some cheese, bread and some cheap wine before booking in.

The double room was clean with a separate toilet and shower room, and Romancia immediately collapsed onto the bed as I opened the French window that looked out into a central hotel courtyard and breathed in that linen and cheap perfume smell so typical of Parisian back streets at night when the hookers are at work. I ate some bread and cheese, and opened the bottle of wine, lighting a cigarette as I did so. Turning to Romancia,

"Welcome to Paris", I said

"Thank you for bringing me here", she replied, breathing in deeply. "I am going to have a good time, I know it. And it should be a wonderful place to become the wind of love. It is a city of love after all"
"Is it?"
"It will be"

The next day, neither of us woke up before midday, and I decided that we were going to have a very lazy day doing very little. We would still have nine days left after all, and I felt that certain things about Paris as it was today needed explaining.

"What does Paris mean to you Romancia?", I asked
"It means Nôtre Dame, and the Seine separating the university from the town", she replied.

Those distinctions are still there of course, but modern Paris has of course moved on a pace since Romancia's time. I realised I was going to have fun with my history lessons, and as Romancia continued to lie there on the bed I also realised that I was in danger of falling in love with her if I wasn't careful, something I didn't want to happen. I wanted in all honesty to be able to meet Leonardo again and say nothing of any kind had passed between us.

But on that first day we did indeed do very little, except do that most Parisian of things and go and frequent the many cafés that existed close to the hotel down the local side streets. I love sitting in Parisian cafés, and Romancia didn't seem to mind either. I decided to start my history lessons there and then.

"The first thing we will do tomorrow is go to the Louvre", I said
"We can't go to the Louvre", replied Romancia, "it's the royal palace"
"It was the royal palace, but now it is public art gallery. The Bourbon monarchy actually left the Louvre anyway under Louis XIV, the so called Sun King, and moved to a palace out of town called Versailles, for fear of mob insurrections, but that's almost another story. The point is that the revolution of 1789 changed the European political world forever, and the Parisians have been good at revolutions ever since. There was another one in 1793, another one in 1830, another one in 1848, and another one, almost, in 1968. But the Bourbon monarchy was essentially kicked out in 1789 when the original revolution began, heralding the Rights Of Man, something, by the way, it has just occurred to me that Leonardo and Michelangelo may well have had a hand in, but I've never asked them"
"The Rights Of Man? What about the Rights of Women?"
"Well, actually, there was one of those as well, written by a woman called Olympe de Gouges, but I've never been able to find that much out about her. I do however, have a copy of the speech at my house"
"That's a shame", said Romancia, "I shall never visit it"
"Why not?"
"Because at the end of our time here, I shall vanish and become the wind of love itself. And only then will I find Leonardo, or tell him I still love him. I shall wrap the wind of love around his ears"

At this, Romancia proceeded to blow on the café lampshades, making them motion from side to side. The shadows in the café went into animated relief. The barman looked up at me, and I put my hand to the lampshade above our table and held it to steady its movement.

"Pardon", I said
"Merci. S'il vous plaît", he replied
"Don't do that again", I said to Romancia
"I won't do it so blatantly", she promised. "I was just testing my powers. I have always had an affinity with the wind, Michael"

I attempted to light a cigarette. Romancia blew out the lighter flame.

"Stop it", I said, almost laughing. "Everyone will watch us, or rather me, the only one they can see, and we'll get kicked out"
"I'll stop then", said Romancia. "Light your cigarette, and continue"

I did so.

"The French revolution was the beginning of modern European democracy and freedom. It was in many ways too much too soon, but it has left lasting legacies. It had its heroes, such as Danton and Marat, and ultimately its villains, such as the bloody Robespierre and ultimately the military genius but flawed man Napoleon Bonaparte, who betrayed the revolution by starting his own new monarchy and declaring himself to be the Emperor in 1803. But there are good things about Napoleon as well of course. The legal Code Napoleon for one, and his attempts to unite

Europe as one political entity have a logic to them as well"

" Gosh, what a story"

"Oh, the story is an epic one, but the point today, or rather tomorrow, is that we shall visit the Louvre as a public art gallery, and see a great deal of French post-revolutionary art. So at least the revolution succeeded in making a royal palace a public space"

"I see"

"And France is now a republic, and you must know what a republic is, because the Romans once had a republic, and Venice was a republic when you were alive, was it not? And we will visit Versailles whilst we are in Paris as well. I never have done, and it would be interesting to see how the Sun King saw himself"

"A Sun King?"

"Yes, Louis XIV called himself the Sun King, and also Louis Le Grand by the way, but that title has never quite stuck. He lost the war of Austrian succession after all"

"Tell me more about this man the Emperor Napoleon"

"He was a great military genius, but he understood nothing about sea power, and lost the battle of Trafalgar to the English in 1805. The revolution however created many land wars, which Napoleon mainly won until finally overstretched. Napoleon was also a Corsican child of the sun and didn't understand freezing temperatures. So he came very unstuck when he invaded Russia in 1812"

"Napoleon invaded Russia! But Russia is vast"

"And very cold. Hitler made the same mistake in 1941 with the Nazis"

"Hitler. Ah, ha, I have heard of him. He was not a person. He was actually a devil. Many Nazis were. I've

met quite a few. But they never tell you anything other than they rule the world"
"They don't. They were all defeated in 1945. Since which time, democracy and freedom have triumphed, but if you really believe that, you will believe anything"
"I am not interested in the world as it is today. It will all vanish in time. But I am interested in the French revolution. If you say it is important, then it must be. And what is this about a Sun King? Do you think there is a Sun God?"
"Leonardo is convinced there isn't"
"And Leonardo is normally right. But have you met the Sun God?"
"Of course not"
"Perhaps you will. Apollo is a very ancient myth"
"I don't know anything about Apollo"
"Apollo is the Sun God Himself! In Greek mythology…"
"Greek mythology? I know nothing"
"I'm an expert. Not that it ever helped me. But I do know Apollo is their Sun God. And the sun is the sun"
"What do you mean by that?"
"As Leonardo must have pointed out to you, it is the ultimate energy source of everything. So it has to be understood"
"Leonardo now thinks it is all about nuclear fussion Romancia. A kind of energy that is almost infinite, but I can't really explain more. But we have penetrated the sun now beyond the myth of Gods"
"Perhaps. And perhaps the Sun God would welcome the wind of love. A wind of love that blessed honest lovers"
"You're serious about this aren't you?"

"Totally. We shall have our ten days in Paris, and we will fall in love as well. I feel very privileged to be with you"

"The privilege is all mine"

"But then I will vanish. I know how the wind works. It is my secret. And my own myth which I shall reveal only to the star-crossed"

At this point two Japanese tourists walked in, one carrying cameras, the other talking on a mobile phone. Now Romancia had had land telephones explained to her whilst on Adelphi ward because of the public payphone, but the mobile made her startle. And it was so small that at first Romancia thought the Japanese woman who owned it was simply talking into her own hand.

"How does it work?!", she asked.

"By radio signals of some description. And satellites come into it as well", I replied. "I think"

"Satellites?"

"Yes. Essentially radio transmitters that exist in space. But Leonardo is the one to explain all these things to you. He knows everything"

"I shall never see Leonardo again Michael. If I met his spirit, I would become too corporeal to ever be the wind of love. He understands"

The camera then flashed as the Japanese man holding it, presumably the woman's husband or girlfriend, took a picture in the café. Photography was another thing I realised I would have to explain to Romancia, and with it modern art.

"Cameras take images of people, or anything else, like portraiture", I explained. "Light is exposed onto a chromatic film. Again, Leonardo is the one to explain..."

But I couldn't really get away with saying that twice, so I found myself drawing a picture of a camera aperture and lens for Romancia, before realising that concerning the rest of it, I was out of my depth. And as for digital photography (and the Japanese man was actually using a digital camera!), I decided to leave that out of it.

"We must also go to the Musée d'Art Moderne, I went on. Photography totally changed the traditional role of painters from the middle of the 19th century onwards. It's impossible for me to explain modern art, but you must see some Picassos, and some Kandinskys. His blues are amazing. There is a thing in the 20th century called abstract art. It is art outside or beyond figurative representation, and Kandinsky is a wonderful example"
"I have no real idea where I am", remarked Romancia, "but I am enjoying myself. And you are right. There are so many cars. Too many to move"
"Yes. And this is only a side street. Tomorrow we will walk around the centre and you'll see far more. The Parisians drive like maniacs"
"Where else will we visit? Is Paris now so vast?"
"Yes, vast, but not as vast as London. The Louvre, Versailles, Monmartre, Fontainebleau, Les Halles, the Pompidou Centre, I'm sure we'll see all of those. The best way is to walk, but we can also take the Metro"
"What's that?"
"It's all underground, almost like..."

"Hell perhaps", laughed Romancia.
"It's like big cars under the city, but they are called trains, that's all. Yet more technological triumphs of modern times"
"Perhaps I preferred my time"
"Perhaps I would too. To have known Leonardo in person…"
"You still know him in person. Effectively. And Michelangelo too, who I never met. Leonardo never allowed me to because the public myth of their rivalry was so important to maintain"

I finished my coffee. We wandered back to the hotel, me stopping for more bread, wine and cheese. And some fruit too, remembering to eat fruit always being one of my weak points. As is remembering to take medication, but I had the Clozaril with me, and took it every night in Paris without fail. The above are only fragments of our conversation on that first day, and I felt very tired of explaining things, Romancia very tired of listening to explanations. We fell asleep early that night, the cheaply perfumed air still blowing through the open French window. It was no more than half past nine at night.

The next day we woke early to the sound of rain falling on the courtyard outside our open window. Romancia looked out on it, one of those Parisian scenes that are tatty and dishevelled yet still confident in their late 19th century grandeur. The traffic could be heard from the Paris of the early morning rush hour.

"Everything is so noisy", she said.
"Yes"

"And how many people live in this city now? I can't have any idea"
"About five million in all, although it depends on what you call Paris. I think those are the figures within the Périphérique. The ring road"
"Five million people? When I was alive there weren't five million people living in the whole of Italy! How many people live in London?"
"About nine million"
"And how many in Macclesfield?"
"About sixty thousand"
"That's about the same number as lived in Venice when I was young"
"You were brought up in Venice?"
"My father was from Venice. But the past is not important to me. Only the future"

I was curious about Romancia's past, but it was obvious I wasn't going to get very far. Her immediate past being in Hell, she doubtless wanted to forget all about it.

It was still raining after I went down to the hotel lounge for breakfast, so I bought a cheap umbrella from a side street store and then returned to our bedroom. Romancia was in the shower.

"How did you turn it on?", I asked
"Oh, I can do almost anything. My spirit is incredibly strong. This is wonderful!"

The water washed down her, making no detours for her spiritual contours, yet her contours could still clearly be seen.

"Am I visible to other people?", she asked.
"No"
"Are you sure?"
"Yes"
"Then I could go out naked!"

The thought embarrassed me.

"Hardly. You might get cold, and besides, we might meet our spiritual protectors today. Whoever they are, they are obviously very important, and you don't want to be naked for them"
"No. Have you no idea who they can be?"
"Only that I imagine they must be artists of some kind if they are known to Leonardo and Michelangelo. Come on. The best way to see Paris is on foot, so let's go to the Louvre"
"A palace as an art gallery. I can't wait"
"I want you to see the French Romantic art the most. Painting has moved on a lot in subject matter since *The Last Supper* and the *Sistine Chapel Ceiling*"

So off we went, walking down the Boulevard de Bonne Nouvelle and on to the Boulevard St. Denis where I discovered a tatty bookshop selling old Hollywood poster postcards, of which I bought dozens. *Angoisse* starring Ingrid Bergman, *High Noon*, *Les 39 Marches*, *La Reine Christine* starring Greta Garbo. Romancia was fascinated as I explained that cinema was like television but the screen hugely bigger, and that the act of going to the cinema, unlike the act of watching television, was a public not a private one. Then we turned right onto the Boulevard de Sebastopol and right again onto the rue de Rivoli, reaching the Louvre in about half an hour. Romancia was enthralled.

"The palace of the Kings of France itself", she said.

But the first thing that enthralled me was the big glass pyramid atop the underground shopping centre that now stands in the middle of the Louvre main courtyard, which hadn't yet been built the last time I had been to the Louvre, which I think was in 1986. The pyramid is like no other architectural structure I have ever seen, and also has a series of six triangular fountain pools to keep it company. The sun had come out by this time, and tourists and Parisians alike bathed their feet in the fountains as gendarmes glided by on rollerskates.

"Where am I?", said Romancia, amazed.

And I was thinking much the same thing. This first experience of seeing the pyramid was surreal, and it succeeds in making the environment of the Louvre feel very 21st century. All throwbacks to the ambience of the *ancien regime* are subverted.

"Pyramids", said Romancia. "Somewhere on our journeys here darling, we will come face to face with ancient Egypt"

Romancia's prediction passed me by, but her use of the word "darling" did not. Somewhere my heart jumped, and then I disciplined myself as I remembered that as far as I was concerned I was still only the escort of Leonardo da Vinci's girlfriend.

I bought a ticket, and we went inside the Louvre, entering, as you now do, through the pyramid itself. Art galleries, whatever the good of their intentions, are not actually places that usually inspire me, but there is something so vast and comprehensive about the Louvre that it does inspire awe. However, I am hopeless at reading gallery layouts, and simply took the main stair case upwards, and wandered through many galleries of art and sculpture of many cultures in a wayward and haphazard manner before finally coming to a considered rest in the Galerie Mollien, a sculpture gallery dominated by Michelangelo's twinned pieces *The Rebelling Slave* and *The Dying Slave*. But strangely, knowing Michelangelo myself, apart from admiring their technical skill and the muscularity of the slaves, these sculptures didn't particularly impress me. They weren't what I wanted Romancia to see, and she, instantly recognising them as Michelangelo's, seemed to feel the same way.

"I know of these pieces", she said. "I want to see new things. Look at that! An angel is making love to a woman! How amazing!"

Across the gallery I discovered was the Antonio Canova sculpture *Cupid and Psyche* (1793), which can be described as Romancia saw it. Cupid is of course male, but I thought of myself, a man, making love to a female angel myself! Somehow, the sculpture made the whole situation seem more possible. An angel was only a human being with wings after all.

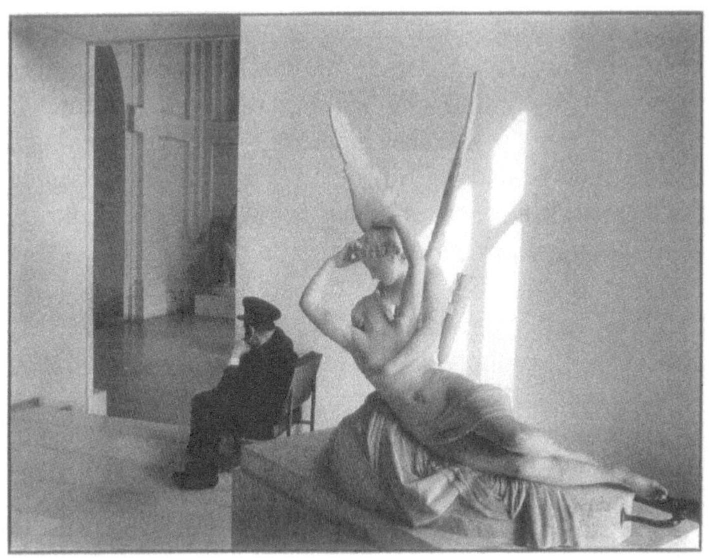

Romancia walked around the sculpture several times, saying “nothing so free would have been allowed in my time. Look at the way he holds her breasts, look at the way her neck yearns for his kiss”.

We moved on, somehow still wondering from gallery to gallery, before realising we were in fact moving with the crowd, seemingly towards one inexorable point, but we did not know to where. Eventually we were simply in a queue, waiting it seemed to view a particular painting, but we still didn’t know which one. And then it became obvious. We were queuing to see the *Mona Lisa* as it is called in English, by Leonardo da Vinci himself. I became aware of this before Romancia, and decided not to tell her. Had she ever seen the painting before? Would she recognise it? Would she have her own explanation of it?

Eventually we were in the *Mona Lisa* gallery itself, and my immediate feeling was one of immense disappointment to see that the canvas is in fact so small, tiny even. It is also very difficult to see properly, having a sheet of bullet proof glass in front of it. Tourists surrounded it from every angle.

"Oh, no, that's not here is it!", cried Romancia. "My God! That's my mother, and Leonardo always hated it"
"Why's she smiling?"
"Well is she smiling? Her face always had that repose. My mother was always trying to keep us apart, being very high born. And now, five hundred years after I'd completely forgotten her, I see her again! How strange"

And then I noticed something else, namely that in French the *Mona Lisa* is in fact called *La Joconde*, meaning *the joke*. But what is the joke? Well, I certainly can't see one, unless it is the supposed smile itself, and Romancia couldn't see one either.

"Other than I don't think it's a very good painting, and it's not even a particularly good likeness. Perhaps Leonardo had other ideas in mind for it he has never told me of", she said. "He could be very secretive about his work"

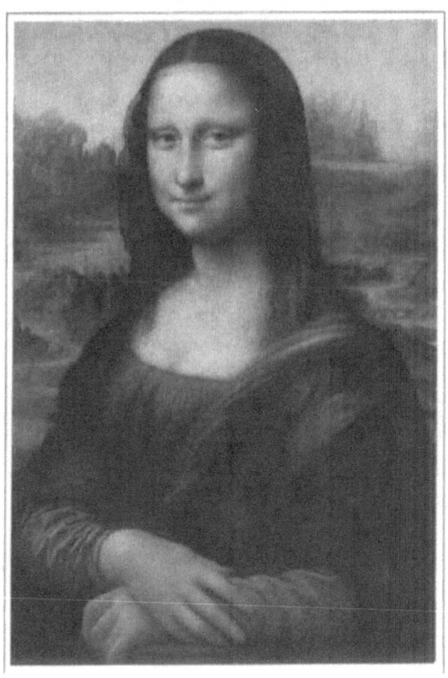

Feeling thoroughly disappointed by *La Joconde*, although intrigued to know it represented my companion's mother, we moved on, and my impatience to show Romancia the French romantic galleries took hold. I even looked at a plan of the building, something in my frequently haphazard ramblings I very seldom do! The paintings I had brought her to see were Jacques-Louis David's *Napoleon Crowning Josephine*, Théodore Géricault's *The Raft of Medusa* and Eugène Delacroix's *Liberty Leading The People*, all vast canvas, metres across.

The David is the largest canvas, and represents the moment when, in essence, Napoleon betrayed the

French revolution of 1789 by crowning both himself and Josephine as Emperor and Empress.

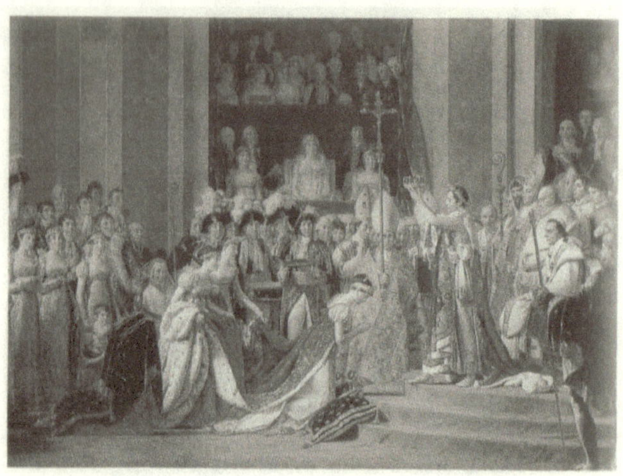

Romancia stared at the canvas and then started laughing.

“Well, I can see who Napoleon and Josephine are, but that’s the Pope holding the Cross up between them! How is the Pope in the picture?”
“Napoleon forced him to show up. I can’t remember exactly how, but he surrounded some Papal land or other”
“Some revolution Napoleon believed in then! The Vatican are our sworn enemies”
“Quite so. But I still believe in the French revolution. And I think Leonardo does too”
“And Josephine looks like she’s being subjugated”
“I think she was. Napoleon divorced her eventually because she was barren, and married Marie-Louise of Austria in 1810. It’s the exact act of the coronation of

Napoleon that made Beethoven cross out his dedication to Napoleon in his 3rd Symphony"
"Is that the piece of Beethoven you listened to on Adelphi ward?"
"No, that's the 5th Piano Concerto. But there are similarities"

We moved on to the Géricault.

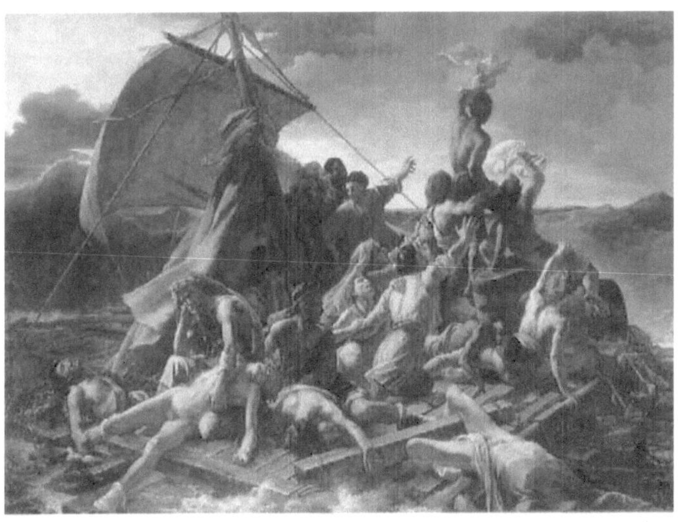

"Now this to me is a truly revolution painting, I explained, and the start of the real romantic tradition of protest against tyranny. The painting had no commission, and came out of Géricault's anger when the crew of the *Medusa* frigate were abandoned off the coast of Senegal in 1819, eighty six of them in all, on a single raft whilst the royalist captain and officers commandeered all the life boats for themselves. Post-Napoleonic France was rocked by the political scandal and the way it revealed the continuing callousness of the

ruling class. Fifteen survivors of the raft were eventually picked up alive by the *Argus*, which can only be seen as a dot on the horizon"
"Yes, but look at the muscularity of the figures, said Romancia. They look like Michelangelo sculptures we saw earlier. Géricault must have been under the influence"
"Undoubtedly. As was Delacroix, who was a huge Michelangelo fan, believe me. Now look at *Liberty Leading The People"*

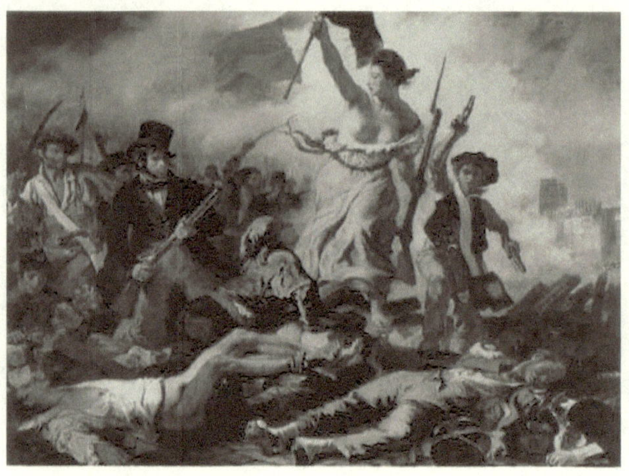

"You see, Géricault taught Delacroix, who was slightly younger, and both were children of the revolution. But forget the history, and look at the angles and composition of both paintings. *Liberty Leading The People* in compositional terms is almost *The Raft of Medusa* viewed from the front, with Liberty's arm raised tricolor, the French revolutionary flag, echoing both the mast of the raft and the torn clothes of the sailor who waves them in the air to attract attention. And the dead and the dying litter the floor of both paintings in similar colours. And again, there is a Michelangelo muscularity to all the figures. And again, Delacroix painted *Liberty Leading The People* as an independent human being without commission to represent the July days of the 1830 revolution when the restored post-Napoleon Bourbon monarchy of Louis XVIII was overthrown. Delacroix is actually in the painting as well. He's the figure holding the musket to the left of Liberty, obviously a street girl of some description, with his top hat on, which must be some kind of reference to the fact that Delacroix took no active part in the July 1830 revolution and was actually in hiding. But no one has ever got to the bottom of that… And please don't forget that Liberty is wearing the Phrygian cap of the Jacobins on her head, the Jacobins being the original French revolutionaries of 1789. Delacroix is nailing his colours to *Medusa*'s mask with this painting, and that of the continuing French revolution in general"

"Which painting is the one you prefer?"

"I don't think you can choose one without the other"

"They are both absolute masterpieces. And not a religious reference in site! You are right! Painting has certainly moved on. The idea of an artist free to work to his own consciousness. That's incredible! You know. I know who the two spirits are in Paris who we will meet Michael"

"You do?"

"Yes. Did Géricault and Delacroix work here?"

"Yes"

"Then it will be them"

"If only…"

"Who else can it be? They must be brave and fearless men to ever have considered painting these canvases, and only the bravest and the most fearless artists would be considered by Leonardo and Michelangelo as worthy of their association"

"If only it could be them. I have so many questions to ask them. Particularly Delacroix"

"It will be them. You will see. Come, let us go. I have seen enough great art for one day and would like to see the Seine"

"And I want a cup of coffee, and a beer or two"

So we left the Louvre, and I took advantage of the fountain pools to bathe my own feet in briefly, which seemed to be the *de rigeur* thing to do.

And then we moved on. We walked west along the rue de Rivoli towards *Samaritaine* and the Avenue des Champs Elysées at first, before finding a café on the relative back street of the rue Saint Honoré. I ordered a café au lait and a Stella and we sat *au terrace* in the summer sunshine. Romancia said nothing, only to repeat that she was sure we would meet the spirits of Géricault and Delacroix before too long, but by this time I was thinking of other things. There was a postcard stand in the café of a dark tanned very attractive woman walking down a red hotel corridor, and the caption simply said *Suite 706*. I took a couple of them, wondering what it could possibly mean, for there were no explanatory notes on the back, but it seemed to refer to some Parisian artistic event currently happening. Perhaps a performance art exhibition, perhaps a CD coming out, I didn't know.

"Whatever it is, that's an attractive woman surrounded by Hell", said Romancia. "Look at all that burning red"

I finished the café au lait and beer and we walked through the Tuileries Gardens to the Quai des Tuileries bordering the Seine itself. We crossed the Pont de la Concorde and were soon at the Quai d'Orsay, home to the French Foreign Ministry to this day. After that we walked down the Boulevard St. Germain and gradually got lost amidst the sights and smells of the left bank…

I have no idea what else we did the remains of that second day, or for that matter the third or fourth or fifth. Time exists in different dimensions when you are on holiday, there is no rush and it seems to slow down, although in many ways it actually speeds up as you lose consciousness of it. "Gosh, is it that time already! We've done nothing today!", for example is a statement that in a working environment would quickly get you sacked, but on holiday it's OK. Suffice to say that we got up late, about 11am, spent inordinate lengths of time sitting in cafes and bars (including paying sixty seven francs for a pint of lager in *le Brabant*, next to the Grands Boulevard metro!), and just walked around in the summer sunshine. We saw the magnificence of Nôtre-Dame and the Ile de La Cité, we saw the Panthéon, Opera, walked up the steps of Montmartre to Sacre-Coeur, we did all the usual Parisian things. We did not however go to Pére Lachaise cemetery or the Catacombs, both favourite haunts of mine, since such celebrations of the dead and the dying seemed inappropriate destinations when Romancia was just out of the world of the dead herself. And since money was of the essence, I ate on the hoof, mainly pizzas bought from the Latin quarter, or just the bread and cheese routine back at the hotel.

We did however go up the Eiffel Tower, which Romancia was determined to do once she heard that until it was built for the Universal Exhibition of 1889, the Giza Pyramid had remained the tallest building in the world for over four thousand years.

"Egypt again!", she said.

The Eiffel Tower has three levels, and we went all the way to the top, which, even on a calm and clear day, wobbles (apparently it never wobbles more than four inches side to side, but even so, you can feel it). Romancia thought it was wonderful and rocked in my arms all too closely.

"I don't have to be Leonardo's girlfriend", she said.
"But you are"
"But you can't really be someone's mistress when you haven't seen them – and you've been dead – for five hundred years. Why can't I be yours? Just whilst we are here?"
"Because I feel awkward about it, and you might not meet Leonardo again, but I almost certainly will, and I want to be able to honestly say nothing happened between us"

The view from the top of the Eiffel Tower of course is indescribably extraordinary, and I shall not waste my time describing what a photographer would do much better, save to say that I particularly enjoyed the view north east towards Montmartre. Romancia and I had walked the final stage to the top, but we got the lift all the way down and then walked north across the Seine to the Palais de Chaillot, with its the guilded bronze statues that gleam in the sun like gold.

“They are golden goddesses”, said Romancia. “This place is Paradise”

After that we walked back across the Seine and under the Eiffel Tower to the Parc du Champ de Mars, and we laid on the grass for hours, as if time was eternal.

“I am in love with you”, said Romancia.
“I’m in love with you”, I said, “but there are lots of ways of being in love. And having an innocent holiday is one of them, however hard it might be since we’re sharing a bed. And it will be hard now. You shouldn’t have declared yourself”
“Why not? Leonardo wouldn’t mind. In fact, he probably expects it to happen”
“What to happen?”
“Love making”
“Can a man really make love to a spirit? Or a female angel for that matter?”
“Of course. Yes. Try me”
“Look. I’m not going to…”
“My spirit will wrap around you. You won’t be able to resist me”

And wrap around me it did there and then.

“Stop it”, I laughed.
“Why?”, she said, putting her hand between my legs.
“No, seriously stop it”

I got up off the grass and walked away from her.

"We can't"
"What? Not here. I know"
"No. Not anywhere"
"You could hug me at night though"
"I could. Yes. I could do that. Would that do?"
"Not really"
"It's just a ploy to end up having sex"
"Yes. But that depends how strong willed you are. And I think you are very strong willed. I don't think I've got a cat in hell's chance of getting your cock out darling. And my apologies for being so crude"
"Good. Because you haven't. Let's just be innocently in love. OK?"
"OK. But you will hug me at night?"
"Yes"
"Promise me"
"I promise"

And with that the issue of our relationship was resolved, or so I thought.

Next up we went to the Musée d'Art Moderne at the Pompidou Centre so I could show Romancia some Picassos and Kandinskys as I had promised her. Romancia enjoyed the site of the Pompidou Centre enormously with its exterior pipes and skeleton, and the escalator that seems to envelope you within its tubing.

"Modernity!", she said.
"They call this building post-modern as a matter of fact. But this will explain to you where painting went in the 20th century", I said.

I found the Kandinskys first, three in particular that I remember now.

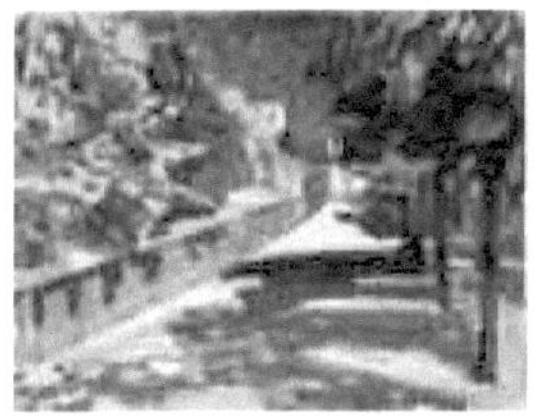

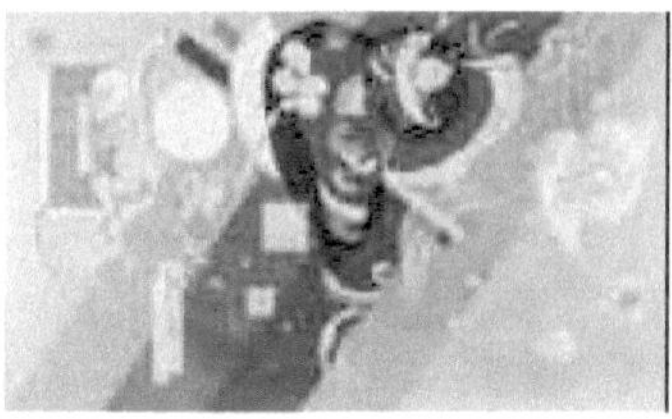

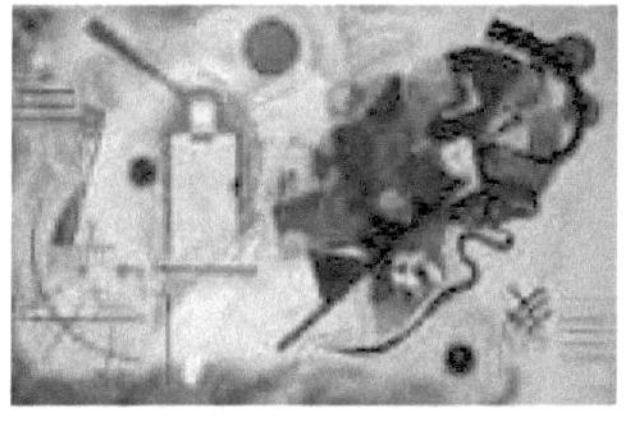

They are *Autumn In Bavaria*, *Composition IX* and *Yellow-Red-Blue*, in that order.

"Autumn In Bavaria is a parkscape, I explained. It's an impression of reality rather than a representation. The other two are well on the way towards the total abstraction of colour using geometric shapes as their guide. And you see what I mean by the wonderful blue"
"All good painters love blue", said Romancia. "Ask Leonardo"
"I know. He explained it to me. What do you think?"
"Wonderful. But I don't know what to say, except to say that religion has vanished again. I can't believe a world can come so far"
"Kandinsky painted a great deal around the time of the Russian Revolution of course"
"There was a Russian one as well?"
"Oh yes, but later than the French. God was banned"

“What a good idea”

I left Romancia looking at the Kandinskys whilst I went looking for the Picassos. But the Picassos tended to be from the blue and rose periods, or like this…

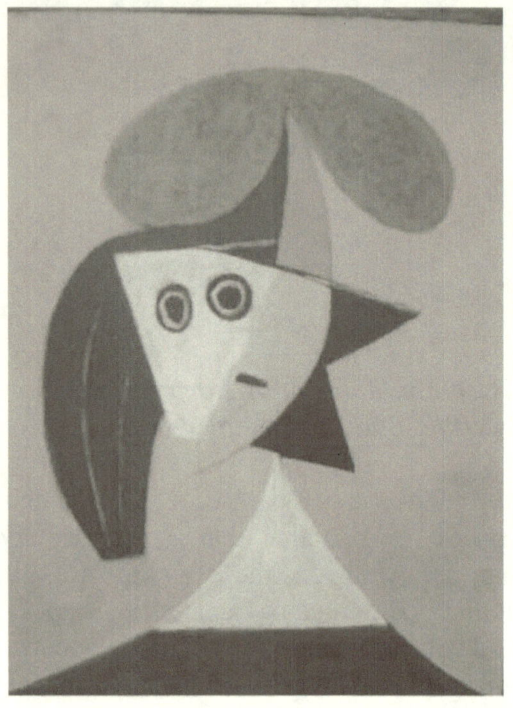

… whilst the two paintings I wanted to show Romancia weren’t actually there, as I now remembered. The first is the first cubist painting, *Les Demoiselles d’Avignon*, which is at MOMA in New York, and the other is *Guernica*, which is at the Prado in Madrid. Luckily, the postcard shop had reproductions of both, so I bought them.

Les Demoiselles d'Avignon I explained is what might be called a brand new way of painting prostitutes…

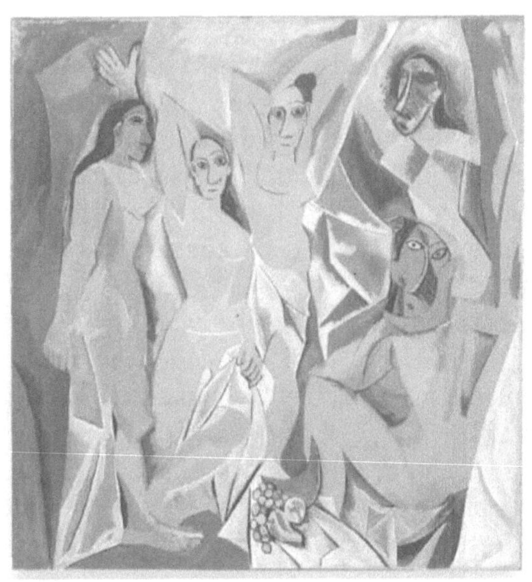

… whilst *Guernica* is the ultimate representation of the ghastly brutality beyond brutality of modern warfare.

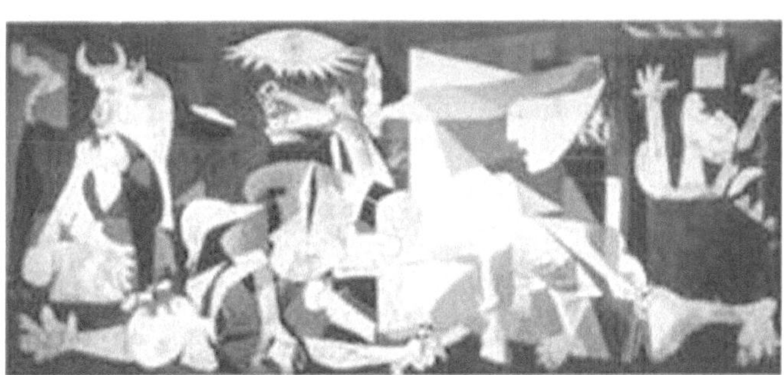

I explained the circumstances of the Nazi Condor Legion aerial bombing of the Spanish Basque village of Guernica in 1936 during the Spanish Civil War as best I could.

"Bombs from the air", Romancia said, "how terrifying"
"Yes, and World War Two was even worse, ending with nuclear explosions over the Japanese cities of Hiroshima and Nagasaki killing hundreds of thousands of people, and poisoning the atmosphere for decades. For many people on the planet, the 20th century was an absolute nightmare"
"That's because God doesn't care any more", said Romancia. "If He ever did. That's why the world is overpopulated as well. D'you think it will end in mass starvation?"
"I suppose it could. Who knows. But I do know that six billion people on a planet this size is unsustainable"
"I only want those who believe in the wind of love to survive", said Romancia, still staring at *Guernica*. "The rest don't deserve to. Most of humanity is depraved, or believe in stupid things such as a righteous and caring God"
"Yes, but our views are what might be called in the minority"
"Our views as you call them are correct darling. Come on, let's go. I loved the Géricault and the Delacroix paintings, but these depress me, even if they are great art, and I can see that"

We got out of the Pompidou Centre and ended up walking around the markets at Les Halles, another monument (and a very good one) to steel 20th century architecture. Then we must have headed south west and kept going for some time, because we ended up walking past the Jardin des Plantes and the Gare d'Austerlitz, where on the rue de Navarre I came across a wonderful shop called Paris Jazz Corner, which sells any number of CDs and records on two floors. However, my bad French proved incapable of explaining my reasons for brandishing the *Suite 706* postcard, and if it was a CD that had just come out, they didn't have it. After that we stayed on the left bank all night, sitting *au terrace* at a cheap Chinese restaurant for hours. At some point I went to the toilet, and when I got back, Romancia was beaming at me.

"I told you", she said, "and it's true"
"What's true?"
"Géricault and Delacroix. They're the spirits come to protect us, that's for certain"
"Then where are they?"
"Look over there"

So I did, and there they were indeed on the other side of the street either side of a small tree, Géricault dressed as a musketeer with shoulder length hair brandishing a sword, and Delacroix dressed, including the top hat, as he is in *Liberty Leading The People*.

"Greetings to Romancia and Michael", said Géricault. "And welcome to our Paris. We have in fact been watching you throughout your time here by the way, but we didn't want to be intrusive. However, now, at this interim time in your stay when you have had ample time to acquaint yourselves with both this city and with each other, it is only fair we declare ourselves. Théodore Géricault. Delighted to meet you"

“Eugène Delacroix”, said Delacroix, removing his hat and ruffling his hair, “like wise. Romancia. Michael. I am doubly honoured”
“And I’ve never heard him say that before in my life”, said Géricault.
“Shall we go somewhere private?”, said Delacroix. “Our revolutionary lair perhaps. Please follow us”

So we did, walking west through the left bank towards the Jardin du Luxembourg and across the Boulevard St. Germain north to a small deserted street called the rue de Furstenberg. We stopped at the door of No. 6, to discover a sign saying Musée Delacroix.

“This, Michael and Romancia, was my last home and the place where I died, and it is now a museum in my honour, as you can see. But we cannot presently go in of course, because it is night time and it is not open. However, let us converse here, no one will see us. It is deserted”

I decided to check my references before the conversation went any further.

“Do you know Michelangelo?, Delacroix,” I asked.
“Do I know him? Who do you think looked after me when I was growing up? Know him!? Both Géricault and I know both Michelangelo and Leonardo extremely well, although contacts have not been frequent of late, or at least not by the time spans of your young life Michael, though Romancia would see things differently”
“Alright then, what are they like? Come on. Tell me”
“Leonardo”, said Géricault, holding the point of his sword up to my nose, “is calm, rational and considered,

whilst Michelangelo is shall we say somewhat sublime. And very difficult at times to be with, his boredom thresholds being so low. Will that suffice, Michael?, and please don't question our credentials again. Once is enough. Leonardo, Michelangelo, Géricault and Delacroix. We are after all the Four Musketeers Michael…"

"Good", said Delacroix, "then let us bring introductions to an end. Romancia, are you cold?"

"Not in the slightest. I am enthralled"

"All well and good", said Delacroix, "for I have much to say"

"But first", said Géricault, "I must explain my relationship with Delacroix. Eugène is in fact the ruler of Paris in all essential metaphysical details. He runs the city, but for the most part on a day to day basis pays no attention to its comings and goings. They are mundane and unimportant"

"Is that why you were in hiding in 1830?", asked Romancia.

"Quite so. I was directing proceedings from behind the scenes. I painted myself in *Liberty Leading The People* because I was most assuredly involved in those glorious July days, but I painted myself in morning clothes because I did not actually take part in any physical street fighting. I have often been accused of dishonesty for painting my part in my own painting, but I consider it to be a wholly honest representation of my role at that time. Thank you"

"Are you Talleyrand's son or Charles Delacroix's son?", I asked.

"How should I know Michael?", said Delacroix. "No one ever told me. But the rumours that I was the slippery Talleyrand's son do explain why there were always

rumours concerning my honesty, despite the obvious commitment I had to my art of painting. But Michael, this is not an interrogation. I had always imagined you would be pleased to meet me…"
"I am, I'm ecstatic!", I assured him.
"… Then call me Eugène, please, and I have watched over you every single time since you first came to Paris in 1982 alone and bought a very big book indeed which was I believe entitled *Delacroix* by Maurice Serrulaz"

Delacroix smiled. I smiled back. Romancia laughed.

"You two have been on each others trail for some time!", she cried.
"Quite so", interrupted Géricault. "But if I may be allowed to continue. Delacroix is the revolutionary spirit of Paris personified, whilst I, no less a revolutionary than he, am his own protector. And it has always been thus. When I was young, I resolved to be the greatest French painter of all time, and was quite convinced I would be so, *The Raft of Medusa* still being in my opinion an absolute masterpiece"
"Well it is", said Romancia, "I have seen it"
"I know. Anyway, there I was, convinced of my supreme talent, when I met the younger man Eugène Delacroix, whose work had an energy and colour that surpassed even mine. I had two choices. Either to be so jealous as to kill him, or to use my greater experience of life to protect him and make him an even greater painter than even he thought he could be. And so, obviously, being an honourable and brave man, I chose the latter path. But there is more to this story than simply securing for Delacroix a junior post in my own studios, which is all

you will read in the art history books. The young Delacroix painted with a gusto that surpassed even my own, and it became clear to me that here was a man so talented that he would incur the jealousy and wrath of God, who would be so jealous of his talents as to send him to Hell without question, a fate I had in fact previously considered to be very probably my own. So, to avoid this fate being inflicted on Delacroix, I resolved to die before him, which I did. I went to England, painted some inconsequential pictures of horses, amongst other things, and gradually wasted myself. Eventually, I recklessly lept over a metal fence and died of injuries to my back aged not forty. Hell awaited me anyway, but I fought my battles against entry, resolving, as I always had, to stand forever if necessary before the gates of Hell so that upon his death Delacroix would not enter himself. And so when he died some thirty years after me, there I was, fighting with my sword against the Devil to deny Him his prize, Eugène Delacroix himself, the most talented man of his time. My fight was epic and I succeeded in my intention of keeping Delacroix out of Hell, and we have been inseparable ever since, and still are. And so I conclude my tale. Thank you for listening, and Romancia and Michael you are both our friends, but if you cross either of us, in this, our city, then you will die"

"Cross you?", I queried. "That's highly unlikely"

"Good", said Delacroix, "so now your interrogations and our threats are over, both. But it is late, and I think it is time for you both to go back to your hotel. May we accompany you? And I suggest you buy some more wine Michael. There is a great deal to talk about, and your hotel is the safest place in Paris to speak at length. *All for one, and one for all!* It has been arranged..."

So we walked back to the rue du Faubourg Poissonniere across the Pont des Arts and around the back of the Louvre.

“Don’t look at Nôtre-Dame”, said Delacroix, “always avert your eyes from organised religion. In Paris Cardinal Richlieu still reigns and musketeers are his sworn enemy”
“I’m well aware of that”
“You must explain *The Three Musketeers* to Romancia. Go back to the Louvre and in the pyramid itself you will find a bust of Cardinal Richlieu himself by Bernini. That is the place to do it. I did everything in my power to stop the bust being put there of course, but these things still happen. What did you think of the Eiffel Tower?”
“Wonderful views, great structure”
“The poet Verlaine thought it a monstrosity, and chose routes around Paris to avoid seeing it. But it has grown on me since its construction”
“Where’s Romancia?”
“Don’t worry about Romancia. Géricault will have her covered. Michael, Eugène Delacroix is honoured to meet you”
“Honoured to meet me? The honour is all mine. Who am I?, after all”
“You are a brave man and a very talented writer Michael, and our future king. Eugène Delacroix repeats, it is an honour to meet you, and in Paris Michael, nobody fucks with me. And people have tried, including Chirac quite recently, but he’ll doubtless deny it. And besides it is a sordid affair of no consequence really. Don’t make love to Romancia”
“I’m not going to”
“But you are still in love with her?”

"Very much so"
"And so am I. And so will Géricault be by now. She is remarkable. But you should try not to be. It will hurt you, your kind of romantic love at your age..."
"I know that, but she is in love with me too"
"And she is also five hundred years older than you..."
"What is my role in all of this? I am the future king? The king of what?"
"The king of the world after the flood in my opinion, but it can wait. Your immediate task is to write the book of our adventures, when they are completed of course. I am looking forward to seeing Adelphi ward"
"You are coming back to England with me?"
"Oh, we both are. Most definitely. We shall escort you all the way. I haven't been inside a mental hospital since Géricault painted his ten paintings of the mad at Bicêtre and La Salpetriére. And that is a very long time ago"
"Géricault painted the mad?"
"Yes, and we must find those paintings, or at least reproductions. Apparently, five have been lost, but that could mean anything. Géricault is heartbroken, so never mention it to him. *Mad Woman In The Grip Of Envy*, it is a masterpiece. Michael, I have often been accused of arrogance. But that is because I will start a fight with anyone who questions my status as the greatest painterly artist of all time. I am the great romantic, the great classicist and the great first modern all in one"
"What about Michelangelo?", I laughed.
"He agrees with me, and so does Leonardo. So please acknowledge this fact for me when you write your book, as I forced Picasso to acknowledge it. My *Les Femmes d'Algiers* was copied by him, did you know that?"
"No I didn't"

“Well find his copy, and put it in your book next to my original. I ask this of you as your truest friend if you will have me as that. We need each other Michael. It is seldom I can talk to an equal”
“An equal?”
“An equal. Your spiritual strength is quite remarkable. I can sense it already. Eugène Delacroix. At your service”
“Michael Black, at yours. Eugène. But I’d still rather call you Delacroix”
“As you wish, but the name is a curse. De la croix. Of the cross! Which cross Michael? I am most certainly not a Christian. In fact, Géricault advised me to change my name for that very reason when I was young. But I left it too late, being too well known by it by the time I decided Géricault was right. The young should always take the advice of trusted elders, but of course they never do, just as you will ignore my advice about Romancia”

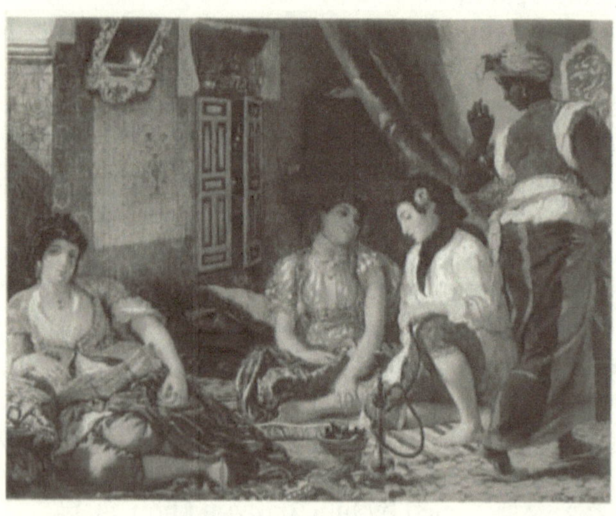

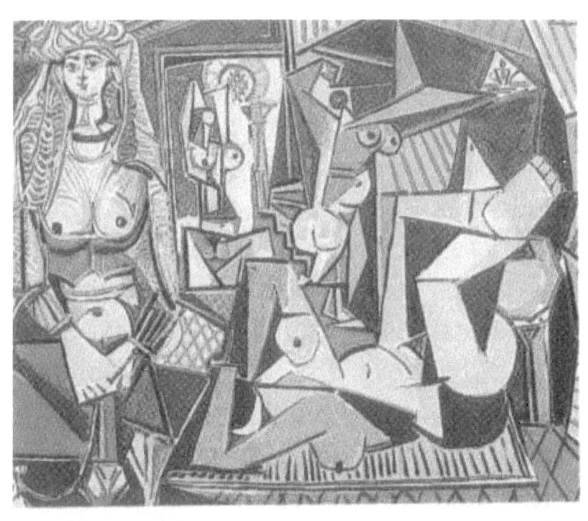

We arrived at the hotel, and I bought two bottles of cheap red wine from the *Alimentation*. It was past one in the morning. I looked around for Romancia, only to find Géricault laughing at me

“Didn’t you trust me with her as her protector, young man?”
“Of course I did”
“He did once I reassured him”, interjected Delacroix.
“So fair is fair”, said Géricault. “Come, let us retire to your room. And don’t use the lift. Stairs are more reliable, and they keep you fit”

So we arrived at my room via the stairs. I opened a bottle of wine, and drank to the health of my three companions. I was all ears.

“Close the French window Michael”, said Delacroix. “This conversation must remain private, for fear of Richelieu’s spies. Has Leonardo spoken to you about Louis XIV?”

“The Sun King?”, asked Romancia.
“The so called Sun King, that is right”, continued my new found friend Eugène.
“Leonardo has mentioned him, yes”, I said. “Michelangelo and Leonardo tried to break into Versailles apparently to find out more, but the force fields were so great they couldn’t get near the place”
“Is that so? Géricault and I have had similar experiences. Romancia, Louis XIV, the Sun King himself, built Versailles as an alternative palace to the Louvre, which he didn’t think was good enough for him. And, so I have been told, it is adorned with images of Apollo”
“Have you literally never been? Not even when you were alive?”
“We both refused to go when we were alive”, said Géricault. “We dismissed Versailles as Bourbon decadence. And we were both too busy painting, particularly Delacroix. Eight hundred and fifty large canvas takes some doing”
“Eight hundred and fifty!”, exclaimed Romancia, astonished. “That’s incredible!”
“Eight hundred and fifty or thereabouts, and I have of course forgotten the vast majority Romancia”, explained Delacroix. “It was in fact far too many. But I haven’t forgotten *Liberty Leading The People*, or *Jewish Wedding In Morocco*, or *Les Femmes d’Algiers*, or *Massacre at Chios*, and a certain ceiling that I shall come to”
“You painted ceilings? Where?”, I asked.
“Be patient young man”, said Géricault, gently chastising me. “All will be revealed”
“Where was I Géricault?”
“You were talking about statues of Apollo”, said Romancia, intrigued.

"Yes, yes. There are apparently statues of Apollo at Versailles, and you Michael, and Romancia must go there. Even Cardinal Richelieu can't stop an English tourist called Michael Black getting away with doing that"
"And whilst you are about it you can take Romancia to Fontainebleau as well", said Géricault. "It is as well to check both palaces, though we don't think there is actually anything at Fontainebleau of interest"
"How many palaces did these Bourbons have?", laughed Romancia.
"Too many. But Versailles is the one, where the entire court of Louis XIV was assembled"
"Statues of Apollo?", I asked. "I'm ignorant about all this"
"Well I, Michael", said Delacroix, "am most definitely not. Michael, what does a Sun God look like?"
"Leonardo doesn't think we need a Sun God", I said.
"Yes I know that. But I think Leonardo is wrong"
"Leonardo is wrong?"

I was dumbfounded. The idea of Leonardo, the great sage of considered wisdom I had got to know so well since York in 1994, being wrong about anything was almost sacrilege to me. Géricault and Delacroix laughed.

"Michael", said Delacroix. "You are allowed to disagree with Leonardo da Vinci! It is not a crime"
"But I thought we were trying to get rid of God"
"Yes, our God. The Judaic-Christian God most certainly. But suppose there is another greater God beyond Him. And if there is, and that god is the Sun God, called Apollo or otherwise, then we cannot get rid of Him,

because the sun is the sun, and without Him, everything would go dark and die"

"So?"

"So I want to talk to the Sun God, after we have got rid of God that is, and strike a deal with Him"

"A deal with a Sun God?"

"The Sun God Michael. There can only be one, for there is only one sun"

"What kind of deal?"

"A reasonable deal. A deal that says I will acknowledge your existence but will not worship you. A deal that states the Sun God treats Eugène Delacroix as His equal"

"But you're not a God, Sun God or otherwise"

"But I have a right to exist Michael. As do all present here. I will not worship Michael, but I will acknowledge ultimate power provided it is not tyrannous. And what if?..."

"What if what?"

"What if the Sun God has lost all patience with humanity, and, through a few hundred years of global warming, plans to flood the planet and start creation again. Because if that is the case, I object"

"And so do I. Strongly", said Géricault. "Most of humanity might be guilty, but I am most certainly not. And neither is Romancia, or any of the Four Musketeers. So, we negotiate with the Sun God to moderate the flooding, most people die, but not us, and then the world is ours, and you are the King Michael of a brand new planet. Simple"

"Simple!?"

"Very simple indeed if we can make contact with the Sun God"

"But what if there isn't a Sun God? Perhaps Leonardo is right"

"Michael, to gain further knowledge, we must proceed on the assumption he is wrong"

"Does he agree?"

"I don't know. Who cares? I'll worry about that later"

"Oh Eugène Delacroix", laughed Romancia, "you have had some arguments in your time haven't you"

"Just a few"

"With Michelangelo and Leonardo?"

"They were once frequent, but not any more. And they protected both Géricault and I when we were young without us knowing, as Michelangelo also protected you Michael"

"So fair is fair. Arguments amongst friends Romancia", reassured Géricault.

"Carry on Eugène", I urged.

"Right. The Sun God. Let us presume He exists and is planning to flood the planet. We must, to survive, persuade him to do otherwise. But first, we must make contact. And to make contact, we must first prove that we are not pillocks who believe in the sacrifice of Jesus on the Cross …"

"That bits easy!", laughed Romancia. "I don't believe this conversation!"

"… and then we must prove that when it comes to the Sun God, we have done our researches and used our imaginations. In other words, we must find Cleopatra"

"Ancient Egypt!", exclaimed Romancia. "I knew it!"

"What?"

"Cleopatra Michael. The ancient Egyptian queen herself"

"Yes, yes, I know that"

"I presumed you did. There were in fact at least seven queens of Egypt called Cleopatra, and I believe it was the same spirit coming back each time, as spirit who

simply refused to die, which, as we know, can be done. Now, the ancient Egyptians believed in the Sun God Ra, amongst other gods, and they built pyramids to secure an after life for their kings which shone of polished stone in the sun itself"
"The Egyptians believed all kinds of things we wouldn't believe now", I said doubtfully.
"Yes, but about the Sun God they were quite consistent, and they are also the first civilisation to become concerned about an after life, which their kings obviously associated with the sun itself. Various Pharoahs who don't matter now had arguments about which was the true Sun God, just as we today have stupid arguments about which is the true god, but they don't matter either. What does matter is that the Pharoahs saw themselves as the living image of the Sun God, indeed Tutankamon actually means "Living Image of Amon", Ra's full name being Amon-Ra"
"This is along way from Apollo. Apollo is Greek"
"But it's not very far from Cleopatra. Michael, what did she know? Obviously, if she had found some way of making her spirit return time and again she would acquire great knowledge, so that by the time of Cleopatra VII, the one Shakespeare wrote about, she was the most famous queen in the world. Why else were Julius Caesar, Mark Antony, and, a long time afterwards, Napoleon, so interested in her?"

Delacroix was animation itself, his questions weren't really rhetorical, he was just excited by his own train of thought, even though he had obviously thought it all before many times.

"What are you trying to say?"

"Well, no one built Cleopatra a pyramid did they? Or a tomb in the Valley of the Kings. All she had was her own mausoleum to kill herself in with an asp…"
"And?"
"And so I painted her, that's the first thing. In fact I painted her staring at an asp"
"I know"
"Good"

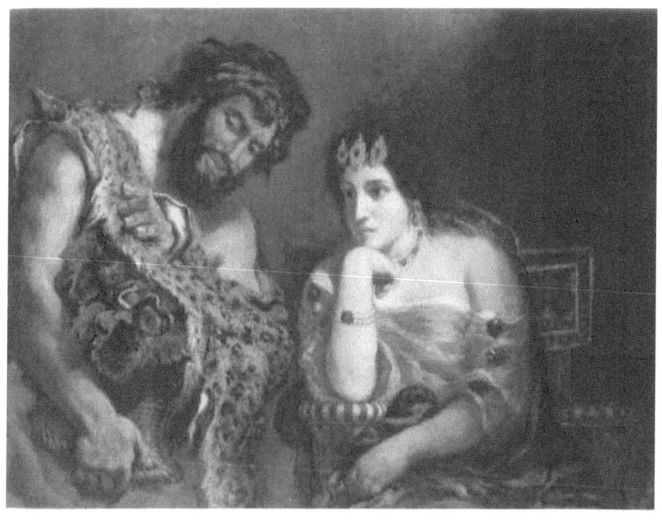

"Now the painting is in North Carolina of all places, which annoys me intensely, but Cleopatra I believe is in Paris, and Cardinal Richelieu knows"
"Cleopatra in Paris? Cardinal Richelieu knows? What is going on? You've lost me"
"It is a lot to take in Delacroix", said Géricault.
"Carry on!", said Romancia.
"To cut a long story short, I believe Cleopatra found the strength of spirit to keep coming back at least seven

times because she refused to worship the Sun God, and He punished her for it"
"This doesn't sound promising. I thought you said you refuse to worship the Sun God"
"I do. So we must persuade Him He was wrong. And Cleopatra must know things we do not. Such as how you get in touch with the Sun God in the first place. Royalty always knows things we do not"
"So where is she?"
"We think she is in hiding at the Institut du Monde Arabe Michael, said Géricault. Not that they know of course"
"I didn't know there was one"
"The World Arab Institute in Paris itself Michael. And that's another building you must visit, and another one neither Delacroix nor I can get near for the forcefields. Allah is at work!"
"Oh, ho", said Romancia, "Islam rears its head"
"Allah is the same as Jehovah and Yahweh, surely you realise that"
"Of course"
"What's Richelieu got to do with this?", I asked, sceptically.
"Well, a cardinal of the Roman Catholic Church, God's ultimate representatives on earth, hardly wants a Queen believing in a Sun God in his own city, does he?"
"But how did Cleopatra get here?"
"Napoleon ransacked Egypt for treasures. She came too. That has to be the answer. It's actually the only one"
"So?"
"So you and Romancia go to the World Arab Institute and see what you can find. Cleopatra is bound to notice you. And all you need to do is express an interest in Tutankamon and find an image of his Sun God funeral

mask to bring away with you. Hopefully there's a postcard you can buy, if not, get a camera. If its there of course, and we don't even know that. But it is a good place to start"
"What good will that do?"
"It will show Cleopatra you are interested in the idea of the Sun God of course, and then perhaps we can negotiate with her, though she must be very powerful, with powers possibly beyond our comprehension. And she's also probably ignorant of western art, so she'll probably think we're all Christians and despise us all"
"That won't be too difficult to change"
"It might be very difficult to change. She probably hates anything and everything European, full stop, and who can blame her? Alexander the Great wrecked the great Egyptian library, Caesar and Mark Antony pursued her to the death, Napoleon ransacked Egypt and in the 20th century the British raided the pyramids. It's not a very impressive record of respect for someone else's culture"

By this time, the sun was coming up and I was tired. Delacroix and Géricault retired and Romancia and I went to bed.

"Give me a hug then", she said…

… and I wrapped my arms around her as I dozed off in much needed slumber, my head at the same time spinning with the scaling nature of Delacroix's plans and imagination.

"The Sun God and Cleopatra", I pondered. "What if I did actually meet either of them? How extraordinary that would be"

"And now we know what else we must do in Paris. It is Versailles and the World Arab Institute for us"
"Yes, and in that order…"

The next day Romancia and I didn't wake until the early afternoon. Géricault and Delacroix were waiting for us outside the hotel.

"There are two other things, said Delacroix. The first is we have found out that *Suite 706* is a CD by Jacky Jayet, and the best place to find it would be *Samaritaine*, on the rue de Rivoli. And the second thing is that you must go back to the Louvre not only to see the bust of Cardinal Richelieu. You must also return there to see the Galerie d'Apollon. *Apollo Vanquishing the Python* is my ceiling Romancia, although I didn't do it in fresco. It's oil and wax on canvas, but it's also a representation, however wrong it maybe, of what the Sun God might look like. A chariot of the sky pulled by horses, although I did think of lions, Leo, and you are a Leo Michael, having its own sun connection. At least we can prove we have shown interest in the subject"
"I'm beginning to think our future adventures would be impossible without you Eugène", I laughed.
"As indeed they would be", agreed Géricault. "But you must go to Versailles now. Be on your way"

So we went, going from the Gare d'Austerlitz that very afternoon, arriving about 4pm. There are countless guidebooks describing the grandeur and elegance of Versailles, so I am not going to here. And besides, Romancia and I had only a perfunctory glance at the palace itself, being awe struck by the hall of mirrors nonetheless, as we were more interested in the gardens, where we knew from the guidebook I had purchased we would find a statue of Apollo lurking in the Avenues and Groves.

First we saw the Fountains of the Seasons, which represent Bacchus or Autumn, Saturn or Winter, Flora or Spring and Ceres or Summer, a reminder, as the guidebook says “that the sun god determined not only the course of the day, but also the course of the year”. And then we came to the Grove of the Baths of Apollo, apparently “the sculptural masterpiece of Versailles”. And there was Apollo in all his glory, surrounded by handmaidens attending his every need. The sculpture is by François Girardon, Louis XIV’s favourite sculptor, and it is most certainly an impressive white marble piece in both composition or execution.

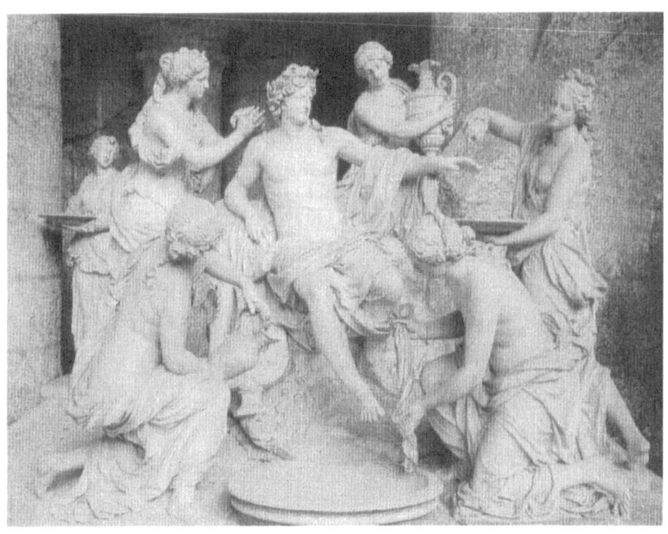

How exactly it represents a being so powerful as to control the Sun I don’t know, but it exists in a secluded grotto surrounded by water and overgrowing greenery.

"So, that's a Sun God", said Romancia. "Obviously very popular with women by the looks of things. Just as you are darling"
"Don't make me laugh"
"I'm not trying to"
"We'll see about that. But at least we can say to Delacroix we've seen the Sun God at Versailles. Mission accomplished"
"But there must be more. Let's have another look inside the palace itself"

So back inside Versailles we went, and were soon overwhelmed by opulence.

"This place is too grand", said Romancia. "I couldn't live surrounded by all this gold leaf. But look, there's the Apollo Drawing Room"

We went in, and saw the circular ceiling painting of Apollo on his chariot in the sky. Unlike the God of Michelangelo's Sistine Chapel Ceiling, this ceiling God looked young and energetic.

"We must see Delacroix's *Apollo* ceiling at the Louvre after this one", I said.
"Yes, come on let's go now. And you've bought a guidebook. But I don't like this place. Palaces should be elegant and functional, not endless celebrations of their own glory. But I must admit, after five hundred years in Hell, the experience of the gardens in the late afternoon sun was wonderful"

I had a beer in one of the cafes next to the palace, and then we caught the train back to Paris.

"How many days have we left?", asked Romancia.
"Only two"

We were running out of time, but it was still possible to do all that had to be done in my opinion, though Romancia had other priorities on top of mine.
"I want to fall totally in love with you", she said.
"And what does that mean?"
"You'll see. And it will be easy"

In the meantime, we went back to the Louvre the next day, stopping at *Samaritaine* first to buy *Suite 706*. Jacky Jayet looked like a good looking woman to me, and I got the distinct impression that Romancia was jealous as I looked at the CD cover.

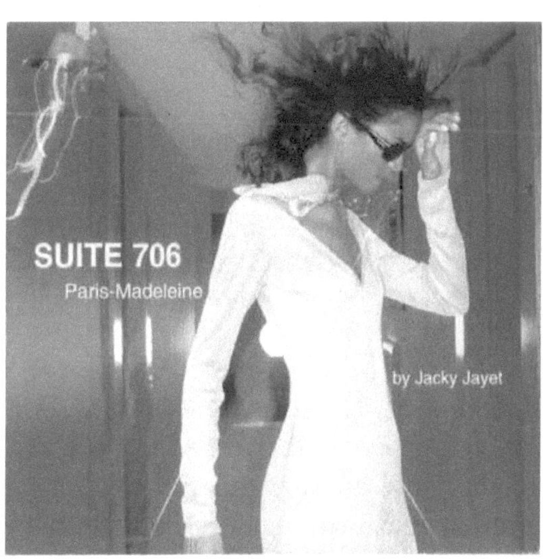

I had no equipment with me to play it in Paris, but at least I would have it to take back to England. The track listings immediately intrigued me. *Grand Tourism*, *Lustral*, *Kings of the Wild Frontier*, *A Reminiscent Drive*…

After that, we entered the Louvre's glass pyramid again and found the bust of Cardinal Richelieu.

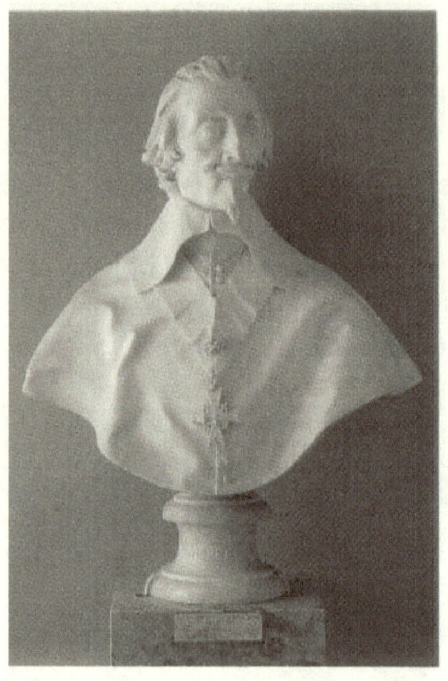

"Look at him in all his grand eminence", I explained. "He is the villain of *The Three Musketeers* and the enemy of the queen. The musketeers, Athos, Aramis and Porthos, and d'Artagnan, the apprentice, are loyal to the King, and therefore at war with the Cardinal's guards, for the cardinal uses them against the King in pursuit of his own power and policies. Meanwhile d'Artagnan's mistress Constance Bonacieux is in the service of the queen whilst an evil conniving woman, Milady, is in the service of the cardinal and plots to kill both Constance and d'Artagnan. Milady it is revealed is also the ex-wife of Athos, one of the musketeers, whom she has betrayed. In the end Constance, the true loyal mistress with the ultimate allegorical name, and d'Artagnan are united in most film adaptations, and Milady defeated and hung. But in the original novel Constance dies, poisoned by Milady. The point being, nevertheless, that d'Artagnan has proved his worth and courage and deserves Constance, whereas Milady deserves to die for she has broken a brave man's heart, that of Athos himself. That's the plot in a nutshell, although its actually very complicated, mixing the affairs of love with international war and diplomacy"

"I see. I agree with that. Dishonest women who break brave men's hearts should die for it. Women should realise they are lucky if they ever meet even one true brave man in their lives, and I have met four. Leonardo, Géricault, Delacroix and you"

"Me? I've done nothing to deserve the accolades Romancia"

"That's not what I have heard. Géricault told me you faced the Devil Himself in York in 1994"

"Well I certainly met Him and confronted Him for an entire night"

"Well that's brave. And it is a brave man who will write your book"

"I have no idea how to do that yet. I don't know when the story ends"

"When you are king of the world"

"That's not going to happen"

“It is as far as I am concerned. And the Four Musketeers”
“But when will it be?”
“It will be whenever you are finally free of the mental health services, whenever that is…”

I remembered I was still on a Section 3! And I remembered I still carried a diagnosis of schizophrenia, which I deeply and passionately resented. There was a long way to go, I would have to go back to England in two days time and…

“I will not be with you”, said Romancia. “I will be gone, the wind of love. I know what you are thinking Michael”

Still, there was Delacroix’s *Apollo Vanquishing The Python* ceiling to see in the Galerie d’Apollon, and hugely impressive it is too.

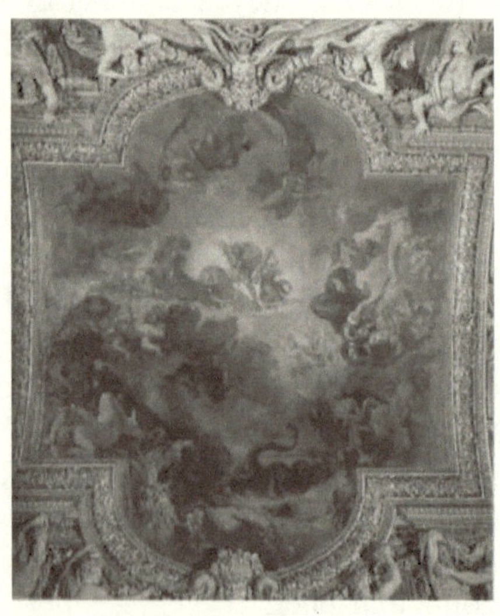

"You will still have Romancia in your heart, darling, though", she continued…

… and with that her spirit entered entirely within my body as I stared up at Delacroix's ceiling. The effect on me was extraordinary. Time and space expanded, the gallery was huge, the ceiling vaultingly high. Somehow, I knew this was a significant victory, but I didn't know why.

"Look what I can do", laughed Romancia.
"I feel dizzy. A Sun God in action", I said to Romancia from within my own head.
"I know", she said. "I wouldn't like to have an argument with him. And look at the power of that sun behind him. Delacroix *believes*, darling… and you are the one who will meet the Sun God in the end. I am convinced. You will be the king of the planet and He will want to speak to you"
"This is getting ridiculous", I said. "Don't be stupid"

At that, we were going to leave the Louvre and walk to the Institut du Monde Arabe, but noticed the ancient Egyptian galleries in the basement, so, thinking of Cleopatra and all that Delacroix had said, we went to have a look. But not for long.

There was nothing about Cleopatra we could find, only many statues in various states of disrepair, all of which suddenly started talking to me. Or rather us, as Romancia's spirit and soul were still entirely within my own body.

"Let us out", they said. "Let us out, Michael"

It was all very disconcerting, and not knowing nearly enough about ancient Egyptian myths and legends I immediately decided to leave, but couldn't find any doors. They all seemed to have vanished. I panicked, but Romancia calmed me down, laughing from within me.

"This was a mistake", she said, "but don't worry. We are obviously in some kind of Egyptian version of Hell and I know the territory. Just find a staircase going up and take it..."

Eventually, I found a Fire Exit and the door was open and we got out that way. We climbed endless stairs and actually ended up back on the second floor before making our way out, taking care to avoid any signs leading back towards the Egyptian statues.

The fresh air seemed to greet us with its own relief, certainly no less than mine.

"That was scary"
"Not really. You should try Hell proper", said Romancia, kissing the back of my eye balls from within me.
"What are you doing?"
"You know what I'm doing"
"Well stop it"
"Why? Today we shall be totally in love..."

We crossed the Ile de la Cité and were soon at the Institut du Monde Arabe on the rue des Fossées St. Bernard. It is unlike any metal structured building I have ever seen, the whole skin being covered by plates of interlocking iris windows made up of interlocking metal blades which move to adjust the size of the central opening, thereby adjusting the amount of light that enters the building. Surrounding the central iris of each window are peripheral irises which are linked to one another and to the central iris. They open and close in unison forming a delicate pattern of light and shade inside the institute itself. Cleopatra, I thought, could be looking at us through any one of them!

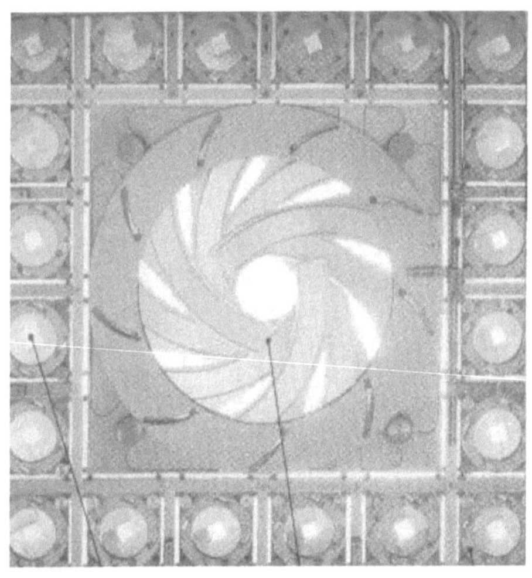

Inside the institute it was actually very dark and gloomy, like the interior of a tomb itself, and we wondered around, Romancia still within me, all the time thinking "is the spirit of Cleopatra watching us? Is she here at all?". But we found nothing of particular interest concerning Cleopatra, and the only thing that caught my attention was documentation of a 12th century poet from Azerbaijan called Nezâmi who wrote five poems, the third one being entitled *Layla et Majnŭn*, which I've always meant to research further, but I've never got round to it.

All of which is another way of saying that we left the Institut almost before we had arrived, finding it disappointing, or disappointing that is until we discovered the bookshop attached to it, which is fascinating. And there we found a postcard of the funeral mask of Tutankamon, a Sun God mask itself. Was this boy king really in communication with the Sun God, or was he a deluded madman? But the art of the mask is indescribably beautiful, and I make no apologies for giving two views of it.

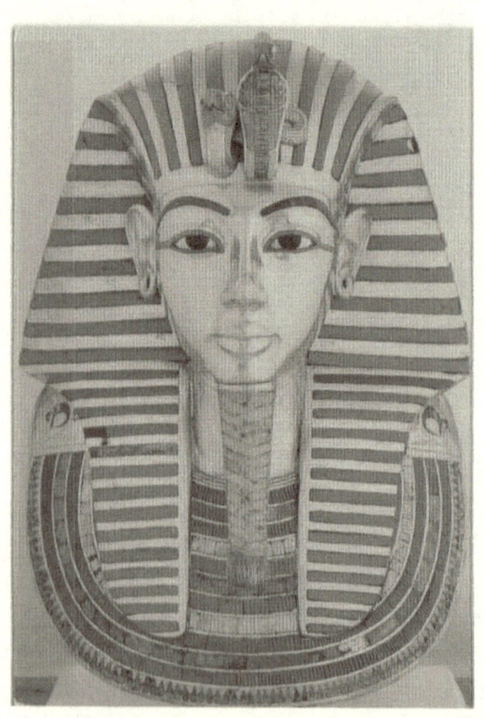

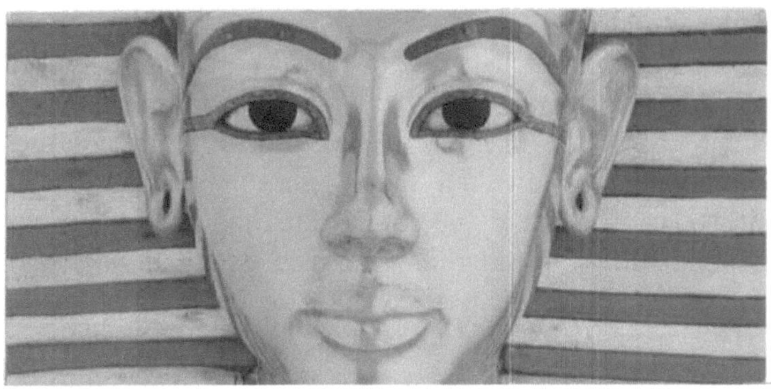

The sheer amount of gold and jade needed to produce it is overpowering in itself. I bought the necessary postcard, and many more of different parts of the arab world, including some advertising Casablanca as a tourist destination during the 1930s before the Hollywood movie immortalised it, and then left.

Delacroix and Géricault were waiting for us on the Quai St. Bernard. I told them of our journeys and triumphantly showed the Tutankamon postcard.

"The power of the Sun God myth must have been incredible at the time", I said. "Wow, just look at that!"

And we all looked. I imagined coming face to face with a Sun God who looked just like the mask. Wouldn't that be an experience!

"But Michael", said Delacroix. "You are both running out of time, so forget Fontainebleau. After you went to Versailles, Géricault and I managed to break in, so our power must be increasing against that of the Cardinal. But there was nothing of interest there next to what you

have found. Only a dirty carp pond full of leather carp and commons. Pathetic. With your knowledge of water filtration you could make the water gleam cleanly and stock the whole place with beautiful koi! Perhaps one day, when we own all these palaces which after all artists, not kings and queens, have built…"
"I think they are all too grand and ostentatious", said Romancia, coming out of my body on to the street.
"That maybe so", said Géricault. "But their importance to us is symbolic. But you must vanish Romancia to be the wind of love"
"I know"
"Is that why you have left me?", I asked, suddenly heartbroken.
"Yes. Goodbye darling. It's been wonderful"

And with that Romancia was gone, her spirit simply evaporating as if into the ether. But then the wind wrapped itself around me one last time.

"Goodbye darling", said the wind through my ears, "and give my love to Leonardo. Let him know I have succeeded…"

There was silence. I felt like crying. I was lonely, my heart bled.

"The wind of love was the point of coming here Michael", said Géricault.
"I know"
"Michael", laughed Delacroix, "you can't fall in love with a girl who wants to be the wind of love! Well you can, but where is the future in it? It's stupid and naïve! But then you are thirty nine and I am around one

hundred and forty years dead. You know the advice I gave you"
"I know it, but it was too late. Why did you two take so long to declare yourselves?"
"We were always watching both of you. But we waited until we were convinced of your merit, which, given the recommendations of our mutual friend hardly needed to be done, but we were taking no chances. Michael! The wind is love! A romantic world is possible! That is success"

So I reflected. Delacroix was right. It was.

"Now Michael", said Géricault, "you shall be the king, d'Artagnan my friend, and you must buy some royal clothes in this city of revolution that shall one day be acknowledged as our capital. So go to the rue de Sebastopol and do so. You will find a shop on the left hand side selling Nepalese pataloons that look Arabesque. They are very world citizen. Buy two pairs, a red pair and a purple pair, and then go back to the hotel and start packing. You have a plane to catch"
"That's tomorrow"
"It isn't Michael. It's later today"
"Is it?"
"Yes. So there is no time to lose"

I did as I was told, buying the pantaloons for sixty francs each, which I thought was cheap at the price. I got back to the hotel, packed, and then ordered a taxi to Opera to get a bus to the airport. Géricault and Delacroix were waiting for me outside the hotel.

“We’re coming too”, said Delacroix, “and if you look down now Michael, you will see a postcard on the pavement with the face and words of one of your biggest heroes on it. *L’Homme Revolté* himself”

I looked, discovering to my amazement, a postcard with Albert Camus’s smiling face on it with the words “Il n'y a pas de honte à préférer le bonheur”

“““There’s no shame in choosing happiness”, Michael”, said Delacroix.
“But I’m heartbroken”, I laughed. “I loved her”
“You should have shagged her Michael”, said Géricault. “But the result would have been the same”
“I could never have looked Leonardo in the eye”
“You still should have shagged her”, repeated Delacroix.
“Gentlemen!”, I insisted. “This conversation will go no further”
“I can see we are all going to get on famously”, laughed Géricault. “England here we come. A new adventure for the musketeers and soon, we shall all be united for the first time ever!”
“Il n'y a pas de honte à préférer le bonheur”, I reflected. “How did the postcard get here?”
“It was just lying on the ground outside the hotel. Really”
“It is a miracle”, whispered the wind, “and yes, you should have shagged me… Thank you for not doing, and I wouldn’t have let you anyway. I remain the one of Leonardo… Romancia…”

The taxi arrived, late by fifteen minutes, but I didn’t care, or didn’t think I did, not realising we now only just had time to make it to the airport on time. I’d had my holiday, I'd been in love, I had my postcard, and I had Géricault and Delacroix too. What a great adventure it had all been!

The rest was simply a rush. We nearly did miss the plane, boarding with only five minutes to go. I sat down in an aisle seat and suddenly realised how tired I was. I picked up the Air France in-flight magazine, opening it at a random page, and there was Uma Thurmann looking ridiculously beautiful and ridiculously like Romancia, advertising Lancôme, Paris perfume. The caption said "Miracle. You make it happen".

Somehow, I knew I had.

Allegro

And choose happiness I decided to do! In essence, two years after this I decided I had finally had enough of my web design job at Stockport MBC (the internal politics were a hornet's nest), and just take the sick pay and live as much as my life on Dane ward as I possibly could arrange. It was gazing at the fish in the fish pond time, it was tea and cigarettes in the Spring sun time, and I thoroughly enjoyed myself, not least of course because throughout this time I was the lover of the angel Jana.

And for the most part I was a voluntary patient as well, a unique status on Dane ward as far as I can ascertain. So I was coming home most days to write *Stealing Heaven From God*, and just using Dane ward as the ultimate free hotel.

But my relationship with Dr. J.S. Bowie went from moderate, to bad, to worse. I asked him to call me "Dr. Black", but he never did, the scientist in him not valuing the artist's doctorate, so I stole his favourite Clozaril mug and started calling him "Joey". The triumph of science is the obliteration of artistic consciousness, but I was determined Dr. Bowie wasn't going to obliterate me! I also read a great deal of psychiatric literature in preparation for what became *Angels, Cleopatra And Psychosis* during this time. I read the eminent psychiatrist Kay Redfield Jamison with particular relish. I read her autobiography *An Unquiet Mind* (in my opinion given the state of the planet everyone should have "an unquiet mind"), and I also read *Touched With Fire: Manic Depressive Illness And The Artistic Temperament*, a book that had a profound impression on me, and one of the best books about artists in general I have ever read. That book represents twenty years research at least!

I started seeing the psychologist John McGovern, in charge of the recovery programme on Dane ward (John has now left, and the programme been closed), and told him I was "touched with fire" myself, which I most definitely am. Dr. Bowie still had me on Clozaril, so I felt fine (until I got neutropena that is!) and life was as good as I thought it was likely to get (until my father was dead that is).

Leonardo, Michelangelo, Géricault and Delacroix were all living on Dane ward with me as well, my house would have been far too small, and we unilaterally declared the place to be our palace! Well, for now at least, no one else was going to give us another one, so Dane ward had to do.

Only one thing temporarily hurt me during this time 2002-2005. I had a bad love affair (with a real woman, not a female angel), and spent too much money pursuing it. The result was I had to get a second job delivering pizzas around Macclesfield in the evening for about eighteen months. But so what? It had its advantages. I learnt the map of Macclesfield for one!

Lastly concerning Dr. J.S. Bowie, I didn't just take the piss. I did try to educate the man! I actually bought him a copy of *Touched With Fire* so he could read it for himself. And nine months later, he had only read one chapter! How unresponsive to the needs of a patient can one psychiatrist get?

Interview with The Sun God

When you are asked, "Where is God? Who is God?", stand up and say, "I am God, and here is God, not as yet completed, but still advancing towards completion, just insomuch as I am working for the purpose of the universe, working for the good of society, and the whole world, instead of merely looking after my personal ends".

George Bernard Shaw, *Major Barbara* theatre programme notes, Royal Exchange Manchester, May 2004

My times on Dane ward passed pleasurably enough, on and off over a period of two years. Generally, I wasn't sectioned, so I was free to come and go as I pleased, and did so, going home most days to write *Stealing Heaven From God.* I was finally taking Delacroix seriously, writing the book the Four Musketeers had asked me to write. I was also more than happy with the angels Jana, Aurelia and Natalia, all with me on Dane ward, and the sun generally shone, or so it seemed. That's about it, save to say I got into Sarah McLachlan CDs, after the nurse Christina Marsh introduced me to her one morning when I was playing Dido's *Life For Rent* in the smoking lounge. Christina knew I liked Dido, so she gave me a McLachlan CD called *Surfacing* to listen to as well. Subsequently I discovered most of the others, *Fumbling Towards Ecstacy* being my favourite. So thank you Christina for the most pro-active piece of nursing I have ever come across. Why don't more nurses interact with the patients like that?

The time I was on Dane ward was spent with us all discussing exactly what we had achieved. God, we were certain, was dying, but the planet, though in a sorry state, was not, and, as if to emphasis the point, my father was diagnosed with terminal throat cancer at the same time. So his time was numbered as well, the coincidence of timing dispelling any doubt in my mind I might still have had about the connection between my father and God Himself. They were the same.

Over the Christmas period of 2003, Michelangelo, high as a kite, managed to ascend to Heaven itself, and, coming down again, told us that the place was unoccupied. He carried with him a metaphysical golden crown he'd found lying on a cloud, which he gave to me to wear on the ward, and then he vanished through the ceiling off to Heaven again. Delacroix assured me the golden crown had been Michelangelo's promise to show he now reigned there. Following on, one day when at home alone in my office, the Sun God appeared before me, a vision of blinding light, and He had assured me He wanted me as the new ruler of the blue planet, before vanishing through the floor. As he did so, he sang a song, *When I Paint My Masterpiece…*

When I got back to Dane ward Delacroix and Géricault broke it to me that the Sun God had appeared there also, and kidnapped Aurelia and Natalia! Meanwhile Cleopatra had also made an appearance, and Jana, turning herself into a poisonous python, had pursued her back to Paradise! What an afternoon I had missed, and one to put us all thoroughly *en garde*! There were many things we didn't know the answer to, but we did know the Sun God wanted me to rule the blue planet and we knew Michelangelo reigned in Heaven.

Géricault, Delacroix and I all agreed that we must have at least partially succeeded in our purpose, although the reasons the Sun God might vanish through the floor escaped us, at least for now. Nevertheless we were convinced we were succeeding in gaining knowledge, however difficult it would be to get Aurelia and Natalia back. But I for one resolved to spend a life time on Dane ward if necessary to do it. This was the start of a new time, a new calendar for the human race full of new opportunities for us, and I didn't care less about anything else. This was the end of the tyranny of science and the new triumph of the artists writ large! That is in the end what gave me the impetus to start seriously writing *Stealing Heaven From God* in the first place.

Life was stable, I was stable, and I even started, however briefly, to try to build a new relationship with Dr. Bowie, having told him of my spirit experiences with Leonardo and Michelangelo, though not about the Géricault and Delacroix. The original two were enough for now! But though I went back to work at Stockport MBC in the Autumn of 2004, with Delacroix and Géricault to return to on Dane ward every evening, I was not lonely, and I even started to consider new career options around the subject of recovery in mental health (a focus I was working on with John McGovern). My mortal life seemed to have more optimism about it than for a considerable length of time. Only one other thing slightly concerned me, and the rest of us. Where was Leonardo? None of us had had contact with him since

Christmas 2003, but then on the other hand we deduced that after five hundred years hanging around with Michelangelo, Leonardo was perhaps in need of a new personal space. Particularly now that he knew that Romancia had succeeded in becoming the wind of love. We all deduced he had gone off on some secret journey of discovery that we would hear about later.

And that is that. I lived a normal enough life for a few months, not seeking out the Sun God or anyone else, nor having any communication with Him. I was waiting for Him to contact me again. And then He did.

On Thursday 28th October 2004 I returned home from working in Stockport at about 5pm. I was met by Delacroix and Géricault standing either side of my front door.

"It's been golden spaceship time today Michael", said Delacroix. "I've seen it land for myself mate. I reckon there's a Sun God inside the house"

"And that's what I reckon too", said Géricault.

"Have you been inside?", I asked them both.

"Not bloody likely", said Delacroix. "We were waiting for you to come back. But we're coming in with you and no mistake"

I unlocked the front door, and into the house we went. My lounge curtains were closed as usual, and I left it that way. Let the light in on a Sun God? What's the point? There he was, shining at us, in human form, but with the head of an eagle. There was no doubt about it. It was Ra Himself.

I fixed Him with a look of serious intent, trying to look calm, but feeling rather nervous. Delacroix stood on my left, Géricault on the right.

"Just a minute", said Delacroix, "I'm going to check out the house".

So Delacroix did just that, and came back about a minute later.

"There's no one else around", he said. "No devils, no other spirits, nothing. Except for Cleopatra in the bedroom of course. And she's your business. Which is good news as far as I'm concerned"

"Me too", I said, looking straight at Ra.

Ra was glowing by now, but not in the way He had when I'd met him in my office earlier alone. If that had been a blinding light, this was a considered presence, clearly come for a significant reason.

"Michael", said Delacroix, this time fixing his gaze on the eyes of Ra Himself, "I want some answers"

"And so do I", I said.

"And so do I", said Géricault.

At this point Géricault went into action with his sword, and stabbed Ra through the heart before equally deftly slicing His head off. Ra just stood there and took it. It made no difference to Him.

"What sort of being are you?", asked Delacroix.

"I am the Sun God. I am Ra. You know that gentlemen. And I am here to explain myself to you"

"That sounds promising", said Géricault. "And we're not backing off you now Michael. Stand your ground"

I had no intention of doing anything else, but it was as ever reassuring to have my two trusty musketeers either side of me. I lit a cigarette, wondering what effect a flame would have on such a divine presence. It had of course none.

"You don't need to play devil games with me Michael", said Ra. "Relax"
"Relax!", I said, suddenly angry. "You kidnapped Aurelia and Natalia. And I'm not happy about it!"
"I can explain that", said Ra. "And I am not apologising. Did I harm them? No"
"Then why did you do it?"
"Because I needed to try them out Michael. I needed to try out their loyalty to you. And I had no need to test Jana because she'd already taken the fight to Cleopatra. And that's brave"
"She can turn herself into a poisonous python you know", I said, enormously proud. "I wouldn't mess around with her"
"I'm not going to Michael. And Cleopatra must have been terrified!"

Ra started laughing.

"I've had a lot of problems with Cleopatra", I said. "But I also Love her"
"And we want to know if you really are the true Sun God", said Delacroix. "And how come Cleopatra keeps saying she's the Sun Goddess?"
"Because she's lying, that's why", said Ra.

"But she says she's got a golden space ship just like you", I said.
"Michael", said Ra. "Have you ever seen it? She threatened you with spaceships landing and devouring the planet as well. Did you ever see any of them? She's a liar, pure and simple"
"I disagree" I said . "Perhaps she's an epic story teller"
"Michael", said Ra, "if you think you've had a lot of problems with Cleopatra, then you should start thinking how I feel! I've had problems with her for two thousand years! And I have finally lost all patience. And thanks to Jana, we can now keep her under control. Wonderful!"
"What sort of a being are you?", asked Géricault, again raising his sword.
"I am Ra. I am the Sun God Géricault. Pure and simple"
"It's your call now Michael", said Delacroix. "We can't push him any further"
"Gentlemen", said Ra, "you don't need to push me at all. I am seriously impressed with you, and that is putting it mildly. And I am not here to play games. Where is Leonardo?"
"We've no idea", I said. "He must have wandered off on some adventure all of his own. No one has seen him for months"
"That is a shame. I was hoping to meet him"
"Well, one day you might", I said. "Who knows?"
"Leonardo", said Ra, "is of course the one who said "we don't need a Sun God", isn't he? I was looking forward to putting him right about that one"
"So we do need you?"
"Gentlemen. You need me. I am your ultimate ally"
"Well I'm not praying to you", said Delacroix.
"I'm not asking you to", said Ra. "I wouldn't insult you like that. And um, Michael, you said to Dr. Lustig on the

phone recently "we don't need a Sun God", and you also said "and if I'm wrong, I'm sure I'll find out about it soon enough". Now, that was a challenge to me, and you know it"

"It was indeed"

"So here I am. You all need me. That is essentially what I have come to say"

"Wait a minute", said Géricault. "Sun Gods, Cleopatra in Paradise and so on. How does all this work? I mean I'm sick of mysteries Michael, and I think we've all worked hard enough"

"So do I", said Ra.

"I want answers!", said Delacroix.

"And you will get them, gentlemen" said Ra. "Believe me. Michael, this is after all your house. May I sit down?"

"Don't say "of course"", said Delacroix. "Make Him wait"

"Wait! Gentlemen. I will wait if you want me too, but time and me are rather bound up together. I could wait for a very long time indeed. It wouldn't bother me. Nevertheless, I would like to sit down"

"In which chair?"

"The blue one", said the Sun God. "And then I can look at your lounge from the most creative angles. I can then look at the painting on the wall opposite to me with the sun at the top of it. I can look at your family collage too, and I can also look of course at the cut away picture of a flying boat. You have been on some journeys Michael. Well done. May I sit down?"

"Yes, you may. Sit down. Ra"

I decided to sit down too, in the small green chair at the other side of the room. The best angle to look back at the Sun God from. Delacroix and Géricault decided to stand either side of Ra.

"Gentlemen", He laughed, "I feel like a prisoner"
"Maybe you are", said Delacroix.
"I doubt that", said Ra.
"Answers, Michael. That's what we want", said Géricault.
"Answers, new questions, new possibilities", said Ra. "Answers alone would be boring for you all I think. And boring for me too. Gentlemen, I am here to cut a deal with you. And I want answers from you too by the way. Such as how on earth have you all survived what you have been through?"
"We don't give up easily you know", I said.
"Let's just call it bottle", said Delacroix.
"I think it is miraculous", said Ra. "It is the most miraculous thing I have ever seen or heard of"
"Really?", I said.
"Really, gentlemen. Your trust in each other, your courage, your ability to always reinvent yourselves"
"That's about comedy", said Géricault. "Comic time is ahead of time, tragic timing is behind time"
"I know that", said Ra. "It is all miraculous to me. You have after all saved the planet"
"I think we've all kind of forgotten that one", I said. "That was the summer of 2001. We've moved on from there"
"Well I don't think you should ever "move on" from that one gentlemen. I think that is the precise point on which you should "stand your ground" as you put it. And the rest follows on. Interesting"
"So we really did save the planet?", I said, suddenly remembering the swirling vortex of vanishing space in

my lounge that Leonardo and Michelangelo had somehow managed to stop whilst the voice of God had thundered on about the Apocalypse.

“You did indeed”, said Ra, “and it follows on, as you know gentlemen, that this is now the artists’ planet. So you should demand control of it loud and clear”

“But no one will listen”, said Delacroix, “that’s still our problem”

“Some people will listen Delacroix. And their numbers will grow. And more people will listen if I agree with you. That is one of the things I have come to say. I think an artists’ planet is a wonderful idea. And it is all yours gentlemen. Well done”

“What would have happened if we hadn’t saved the planet?”, asked Géricault. “Would it have been a black hole or would it have been a barren planet with no atmosphere? And obviously, we didn’t want to find out, but you must know”

“And I do know”, said Ra, “It would have been a barren planet with no atmosphere. I do remain the Sun God, and this is my solar system. It is my invention”

“But it was you in my office a few months ago telling me you wanted me to rule the blue planet in brand new ways?”, I said. “You said that, didn’t you?”

“I did indeed. It was me, Michael”

“I thought afterwards it might have been a devil trick”, I said. “Because then you simply vanished through the floor! Why would a Sun God do that?”

“That’s the one that bothers me too”, said Delacroix.

“The answer, Michael, is that I sent myself to Hell, for a limited period of time only, in recompense of the mistakes I have made in the past. And I didn’t like the place one bit, but on the other hand, a few flames don’t bother me. I survived”

"So where do you live?", I asked.
"I live in, on and around the Sun in dimensions no one else can fully understand. You could say I like a hot climate. And if those morons at NASA send many more space probes up at me, gentlemen, one of these light years I am going to send one of them back extremely fast. I don't like space being cluttered up by bits of human rubbish Michael. It annoys me"

I suppose only Sun Gods can say things like that. Everyone laughed.

"Relax, gentlemen", said Ra. "I am truly your friend"
"Cleopatra", said Delacroix. "Let's start with her. You did say you'd give us answers, and I still need convincing. Because not even Ra can put the sun out overnight, and if we don't like you, then we'll just start a battle with yet another God until we win. I am no ones slave, and I'll learn how to run the sun myself if I have to"
"That won't be necessary. I am the true Sun God, and I am, in my own way, much more powerful than any of you. But on the other hand, this is your planet, the planet you were designed to live on in physical form, and in that sense you have considerable power of your own. Now, Cleopatra. Cleopatra was the one who refused to accept the ancient Egyptian religion of the Sun God Ra. And there were indeed at least seven queens called Cleopatra – I lose count now myself – and in effect it was always the same one coming back. It think, but I may be wrong. She refused to worship me gentlemen, and I didn't like her for it"
"But why did you demand to be worshipped?", I asked. "We'd do exactly the same"

"You could say, from your perspective, that my demand to be worshipped at the time represents immaturity on my behalf. But I would counter by saying that worship is necessary until I am convinced that planet earth has some truly sane rulers at last, rulers I trust, never mind everyone else. Civilisation is a very difficult thing to achieve gentlemen, and my definition of civilisation is a world beyond worship, and has been for a very long time. But anyway, back to Cleopatra. She refused to worship me, and demanded answers concerning the meaning of creation, how the planet and the sun worked and so on, that I simply refused to give her. I didn't trust her you see, and I never have. She has always had far too much ego. But nevertheless, I admired her rebellion in a way – I almost always admire rebellion gentlemen – so in the end I made a deal with her. I asked her where she would like to live, on the proviso that she stopped coming back all the time, and she said "Paradise". In fact, you could say the idea was all hers, so I invented it for her"

"So Paradise is a real place?", I asked.

"Yes it is Michael. It is the home of Cleopatra, effectively above the place that you call Heaven, now the home of Michelangelo of course, and that one gentlemen came as a big surprise to me. I had no idea your ambitions were so grand. So well done"

I suddenly remembered an event from my time on Adelphi ward in 2001 that I had never come to terms with.

"So it was your space ship that landed in my bedroom that night?"

"It was indeed. I was going to beam you up Michael, and take you to other worlds thinking you were far too imaginative to live on earth, but then, what do I know? I had no idea of your own determination or the talent and courage of your friends"

"Well we like this planet", I said. "Or rather we like our ideas for this planet, and we are going to change it"

"I know that now gentlemen. But frankly, in the summer of 2001 when it seemed to me you were just larking around pretending the courtyard on Adelphi ward was a courtyard at Versailles, I didn't think any of you stood a chance"

"Comedy matters", said Géricault. "Comic timing is ahead of time, tragic timing is behind time. As I have just said. Work that out and you've worked out the lot"

"And I have worked it out gentlemen, my difficulty being that I am, by your standards, so appalling badly read. Running a solar system has never left me much time for reading novels, or wandering around art galleries for that matter"

"Cleopatra", said Delacroix. "So her spirit ends up in Paradise. Then what happened?"

"What happened gentlemen – and I knew it would – is that eventually, she got bored of being surrounded by all her hand maidens and lounging around and bathing in milk, and of having sex with the spirits of various men she found attractive, and then – and I will not accept this – she became angry with me for putting her in Paradise in the first place! Well! It was her idea! And that is where all this nonsense about wanting to be the Sun Goddess started. She has ideas above her station gentlemen, and she cannot be the Sun Goddess because she didn't invent the sun. And I did. It is as simple as that, and I have told her so a million times, but of course she never listens"

"She never really listened to me either", I said, "until recently. And you're right about her ego. But then Jana's got an ego too. It must have been some fight between them"

"Yes it must have been", said the Sun God, "and since then, Cleopatra has been very, very quiet. I think the point has finally been made. Being a Sun God is not about conquest, Michael, it is about truth, and the truth is mine. Now, where were we?"

"Let's go back to Natalia and Aurelia", I said, "because I'm still not happy about you kidnapping them"

"And you were prepared to spend a life time on Dane ward fighting me about it Michael! That is what I call guts. But before you get angry with me again – and I can see it in your eyes – please also remember that it has been me giving you energy to survive what might be called your psychiatric nightmare all these years. My energy is the reason you resist so well. As I believe Delacroix has told you, you have been solar powered. And you didn't believe him"

"Well, I believe him now", I said. "So what happened with Natalia and Aurelia? Because they will escape you somehow"

"They will not escape me Michael. But I have already let them go, it is as simple as that. And being as thoroughly convinced of their loyalty to you as I so quickly was, I never intended to do anything else"

"But they will have sworn to escape!"

"I let them go. And this is important Michael. In fact it is all extremely important. Firstly, your love and commitment to them staggered me. I mean name me another man who would be prepared to commit himself to a life on Dane ward just to fight my power once I had kidnapped them? That is the first thing. And the second

thing is that I told them they were on a golden space ship two thousand light years away from home, and Michael, they just laughed at me. “That’s impossible” they said, “we know that the sun is only eight light minutes from planet earth, so you must be lying”, and Michael, I was, and they are also approximately correct. “We love Michael” they said, with absolute loyalty and determination. I fell incredibly in love with both of them as they said so, and asked them where they’d got their information from. And do you know what they said? And this will make you laugh, Michael”
“Go on, I said, what did they say?”
“They said, Michael, that you had looked up the information on the Internet! And I laughed so much at that Michael that I simply resolved to let them go. But to repeat, they did not escape me”

At this point, Aurelia and Natalia both suddenly appeared in the room, one either side of my green chair. Both were smiling, both on the verge of laughter.

“Hello guys”, said Aurelia.

“We’ve had a wild time of it”, added Natalia.

Ra continued.

“Aurelia and Natalia presently both think they travelled back to earth by the power of their own dreamscapes, but in that they are mistaken. I let them go and transported them back myself, making sure they arrived back here in complete safety. And they have to know that Michael. You cannot travel space and time simply through the power of dreams Michael, although it is a good place to start. So I am telling them now. And I am telling them how remarkable they are at the same time"

At this point, Ra got up from his chair and looked at my bookshelves.

"You have some remarkable books Michael. Flying boat books, books on sustainable economics, and of course *The Three Musketeers* in both English and the French original. *The plot thickens!* Gentlemen. This is all a miracle to me. The Four Musketeers are all miraculous to me, as are Jana, Natalia and Aurelia in equal measure"
"Well I certainly wouldn't be here without them", I said, suddenly incredibly proud myself.
"No you would not Michael, and they are of course ultimately their own mystery, as women, angelic or otherwise, should always be. And of course Cleopatra must have been incredibly frightened when Jana turned herself into a poisonous python, and after that I just don't care anymore. Let Cleopatra live in Paradise and get bored! It is her problem"
"I refuse to be bored any longer" came a voice walking down the stairs from the bedroom. It was Cleopatra herself.
"What about God?", said Delacroix. "We want answers Ra. What's the connection between you and God? Or Zeus, or Jupiter, or Jehovah, or Allah? They must be all the same being the way I see it, so what's your connection?"
"My connection gentlemen, is that I created God to create this planet. And yes, all the names of God you mention Delacroix equate to the same being"
"But God rapes things of beauty!", shouted Delacroix. "And this is what I won't accept. And perhaps it was you

after all Ra! How do we know that you and God are not the same being? How do we know you are not lying? Look me in the eyes Ra, and tell me straight that it wasn't you who raped Leda for example. Look me in the eyes, and I'll know the truth! No one fucks with Eugène Delacroix!"

And so Ra stared at Delacroix and Delacroix stared back. It must have gone on for at least five minutes.

"It was not me Delacroix", said Ra eventually. "It was Zeus who did that, and that is also the point where I started to realise that God, to use but one of his names, was going to become a serious problem in the end. Because as you know Delacroix, you cannot have a god who sanctions rape. Civilisation is impossible, women are never safe to explore their own eroticism…"
"And artists can never win!", said Delacroix. "Because female eroticism is where all male aspirations to beauty start"
"I totally agree with you Delacroix. But you, gentlemen, have defeated God, so now your world will become possible, and I am essentially here to sanction your aims and ambitions"

Delacroix stared Ra in the eyes again. Ra stared back.

"Delacroix. I am on your side. And I am on your side too Michael. The geometric dream I gave you on Dane ward over the Christmas of 2003. What did it say to you?"
"It said you wanted me to be a god", I said.
"Correct Michael. And I liked your reaction Michael. You woke up, went into the smoking lounge, lit a

cigarette and started to think about the implications. And I will tell you what they are. I want you to be a new kind of god Michael. A mortal god at ground level, who leads a normal life and tells the story of all your endeavours – and mine too – in your book. *Stealing Heaven From God*, Michael, and that is exactly what you have all done. So well done, to repeat it is a miracle to me. You don't need to be divine and in Heaven Michael. Firstly you are far too young, and secondly, Michelangelo is already in Heaven, and to me that is the biggest miracle of all"

"There's a problem there", said Delacroix. "And to me it is still a big one. Michelangelo has spent five hundred or so years dreaming of being in Heaven, but he won't be happy there forever. He's still a human spirit, and at some point he will want to come back down to ground level. And if he's not allowed to, he will eventually go mad, and then we'll have another god problem on our hands. I know Michelangelo, Ra, we all do. He will get impatient if he's always in Heaven, and demand civilisation be more beautiful than it can be made in real time"

"I've never thought about this", I said, "but I agree. So what's the answer, Delacroix?"

"The answer, Michael, is that I want to be able to live in Heaven too, from time to time, so that Michelangelo can sometimes live at ground level as well. So I need the Sun God's power to get me up there in the first place. So both Michelangelo and I will play god from time to time, civilisation will be made a new in real time, stable time, over the next few hundred or so years"

"Gentlemen. What can I say?", said the Sun God. "I grant you your wish Delacroix. It is if may say so, a brilliant idea. I will give you the power you wish at the

right time, never forgetting that Michelangelo stole the power to live in Heaven from me in the first place. And, as I look at it now, quite right too"
"Creative theft!", I said. "That is our motto, Ra. We are no one's slave"
"And least of all mine", said Ra. "But then, of course, civilisation has to be a world beyond slavery or it is nothing. Civilisation, gentlemen, start thinking about it, and I know you never really think about anything else anyway. It is a world beyond worship, beyond slavery, and also beyond cruelty, lies and deception"

"Then the Four Musketeers are pledged to defend it with all our lives!", said Géricault. "Michael, I'm getting excited, but I still want answers Ra. For example, if you knew you had a problem with Zeus, then surely you are still guilty, because by your own admission, you created Him!"
"I made God – and let's just call Him God – to create this planet Géricault. And he had his instructions. Water, land, carbon based life forms and so on. But I made Him too powerful. I did try to get my calculations exactly right, but in the end I got it wrong, and as you of all people know Michael, He does not like power being rested from Him. That was my mistake Michael, almost at the dawn of time itself – and there is no time without light by the way – and that is why I sent myself to Hell by vanishing through your floor. But consider the situation gentlemen, from my point of view. A God who was not powerful enough would have been a lot worse. That would have been a planetary miscarriage, with no life issuing forth at all. So although I got my calculation concerning God's power wrong, I now make no apologies, having sent myself to Hell for the mistake.

And since God is now fading into oblivion, who any longer cares? The planet has survived into a new age gentlemen, and it is your triumph. I am excited to put it mildly. This shall be the artists' planet, remade over time to be truly beautiful in all its aspects. And of course Romancia is the wind of love! Gentlemen, it is all miraculous to me!"

"Wait", said Cleopatra. "Hello Ra. It is many a time since we have met. What about me? I Love Michael, and he Loves me. Why does everyone mistrust me? I don't think Jana does any more. I have met my match. Michael, can't you see who Ra is? I have sung the creation song of the Sun God to you many times…"

"Hello Cleopatra" said Ra. And then he started singing his song…

"I've long suspected all of this Cleopatra", I said, "but where do we start?", I found myself saying. "What do we do next? I mean, I shall tell you how we work Ra. We sit around my house – or psychiatric wards - thinking of almost impossible things to do, such as demanding an end to all polluting powered flight save for our ownership of five hundred *Solent* flying boats, but we all know that we won't get away with it in practice"

"You will get away with it in practice gentlemen. But it will take time, and twenty or thirty years perhaps, not merely two or three. But in one sense or another you will all survive, as will Natalia, Aurelia and Jana, so the future is yours. I am announcing it for you here and now. But here, in my opinion is both what you do and don't do next. Firstly, Delacroix, you rebuild the Egyptian pyramids so they shine in the sun. Ultimately, that will create more oil, and we do need more oil. Secondly, the Egyptian statues that talked to you and Romancia in the basement of the Louvre Michael. Leave them there to rot. Those statues are the trapped spirits of some seriously evil beings, and Napoleon looting Egypt for some of its ancient treasures is one of the best things that ever happened in my opinion. So rebuild Egypt anew gentlemen. It was once my favourite civilisation, and I wish it to be so again. From Cleopatra onwards, it all went wrong, but it was not her fault, and I defend insisting on being worshipped in that context, because the situation needed controlling in lots of ways, as did the God problem as well, which I was also trying to deal with. Why do you think the ancient Egyptians enslaved the Israelites for example? Need I say more?"

"That makes sense to me Michael", said Delacroix. "So what do we do next Ra?"

"Psychiatric wards Michael. Fight for the interior space of defining sanity and madness in new ways before you fight for anything else. It is your idea gentlemen, and it is a brilliant one. You have been engaged in an epic battle between sanity and madness and the sanity is yours And you have already said that your perfect psychiatric ward is a place of beauty where those damaged by psychiatric treatments can live in peace, but forget those arguments. Consider living in palaces instead, and the ultimate palace is the palace of Versailles itself. How gentlemen, is the planet to be remade if we don't listen to the dreamers and visionaries first, who, as you know, always seem to get locked up?"

"Well, we don't know, do we Michael", said Géricault, "and that is our ultimate point"

"It is indeed", said Ra. "And I think that should be your opening demand gentlemen, and you should stand your ground upon it. You want the palace of Versailles. Full stop. And further, where are there modern glass pyramids, gentlemen?"

"In a courtyard at the palace of the Louvre", said Delacroix

"Correct. And that should be you second demand gentlemen. That the palace of the Louvre is your royal palace. Open to the public and still an art gallery of course, but yours to live in Michael. Demand it, and demand Fontainebleu as well, if only to build your ultimate ornamental carp pond. I know how much you love fish. The foundations of a beautiful world can all be demanded from those three opening demands, gentlemen, and I have thought about this for some time. Nevermind the Winter and Summer Palaces in Saint Petersburg"

We all stood aghast at the splendour of Ra's plans.

"Well, we agree Michael, don't we Delacroix", said Géricault.

"Well, I do", said Delacroix.

"And so do I", said Cleopatra.

"And so do I then", I said. "But I'll still stand my ground on Dane ward as our first palace. Because in the end…"

"… at the beginning, Michael", said Ra.

"… that is where everything important took place. And I had a great time! Let's face it guys, we all did"

"You did indeed", said Ra. "And for that matter so did I. Gentlemen, I like you. I am feeling ecstatic. I like you all. With spirits around like yours, anything is now possible. And it is all surprising to me, because until recently I had no knowledge of any of you at all. God's power was such that He hid you from me, which is why I essentially despaired that this planet – the blue planet that I love so much as I told you Michael – would in any real sense survive. Making contact with you Michael, my arrival as Ra on Dane ward, Christmas 2003, was as miraculous for me as it was for you. I wanted and needed to find out about you all, and I was delighted that you said absolutely nothing, and certainly didn't start praying! You just stared me out, and Natalia and Jana did it too. Wow! Because to honest, until very recently, if the planet survived at all, I was just going to flood the place and start again with fish, and dolphins of course to maintain the mammalian connection"

"So what are you going to do now, Ra?", said Delacroix. "Because if we are to make Versailles, Fontainebleu and the Louvre our opening demands, never mind Saint Petersburg, we need to know"

"And they're great opening demands Michael", said Géricault. "That way we take France, and we two are French after all. And we succeed in invading Russia"

"Forget conventional warfare gentlemen", said Ra. "Just demand the palaces in general. It is the only way to win. Now, the planet is not going to flood over night gentlemen, but sea levels are rising, as you know. And the artic permafrost is melting, Alaskan sea levels are rising, polar bears are no longer hibernating and so on. So we shall see how far this process continues, but the main point is that high ground, moral or otherwise, truly matters, and you gentlemen, possess it in abundance. And you live in a sensible place Michael. You live half way up a hill in a courtyard in Macclesfield. You are not going to get immediately flooded unlike the fools who buy houses at the bottom of the hill on Garden Street next to the River Bollin! And you don't like the southeast of England Michael, and neither do I. And it is actually sinking Michael! By a centimetre or so a year, but that matters to me. And it is overcrowded, vastly expensive, and people sit in traffic jams on the M25 all

day. That, Michael, is vanishing space and time, so let the idiots have it. It is their problem. There are actually people in England buying houses built on flood plain land Michael! What on earth can be more stupid?"
"I couldn't agree with you more", I said. "So, OK, we demand Versailles .That's the opening demand. And let's see how long that takes to come our way"
"It won't be easy, will it?", said Delacroix, laughing.

Géricault laughed too. So did Ra.

"I have a few other things to say and suggest", said Ra, "but it is now the early hours Michael, and you have work to go to tomorrow, so I will be brief. Firstly, if Heaven is occupied by Michelangelo or Delacroix, then they cannot live there alone. Heaven was once the home of gods and goddesses of many kinds before God of course killed all the others off out of jealousy. And I want Heaven repopulated by the new gods and goddesses of many different cultures. You will remain in control gentlemen, but if you are allowed to live in Heaven then why should other cultures be denied? So there will be a new secular divinity of brave men and women, whose souls become immortal through their own dreams and aspirations. What do you think?"
"It's fine by us", said Delacroix. "We are multi-cultural you know. Why d'you think Michael still works in a pizza shop? The boss is Iranian, pizzas are Italian, Bette is Slovakian, Geraldine is Irish and so on"
"I know all that", said Ra, "but Michael, you should give that job up. It is stopping you writing the book, and you have proved your point, so give it up"
"I think I will", I said.

"You will find a new fulfilling future, Michael", said Ra. "Don't worry about it. And keep writing. Who is mad, who is sane and who defines the rules? It is your fight Michael. And I think you should demand Prague also. You went there and it suits you. But then you know that"

"I do indeed", I said, suddenly feeling tired.

"Lastly", said Ra, "there is the issue of Gaia, mother nature herself, and Gaia is simply the souls of women, gentlemen, the ultimate life force, whom you are pledged to honour and defend. So defend her some more, and everything we have talked of will come to pass. Including, at some point, your fleet of five hundred *Solent* flying boats. "Look at that, it's a miracle, it's a flying-boat", and a joke against Noah as well. Flying boats are a new kind of ark. Perfect, gentlemen. Well done"

"I'm satisfied, Michael", said Delacroix.

"So am I", said Géricault. "But will we meet again?, Ra"

"Doubtless. When I feel like it gentlemen. I remain Ra, I remain the Sun God, and I remain more powerful than you. But I don't want worshipping, and let the blue planet be yours. Together through life, gentlemen"

"What's with the golden space ship?", said Delacroix. "How does it work?"

"That, gentlemen, remains my secret, but it is optical illusion of sorts, and of course most people simply cannot see it at all because they are not spiritually aware enough, which is their problem. Oh, one last thing. I know Géricault and Delacroix guard your house at all times, but is it really necessary any more? They have now been doing it for three years, on and off, and they must be getting bored. And what are they guarding it for? Ultimately everything save your notebooks could be claimed on the insurance. So why don't you ask if your notebooks could be kept at the Cambridge University library? And then Delacroix and Géricault could do other things. *All for one, and one for all*! Goodbye gentlemen"

And with that Ra ascended through the ceiling of my lounge and was no more to be seen. It must have been about 3am.

"Well", said Delacroix, "tonight Michael, we learned it all"
"We sure did", said Géricault. "We have a deal with the Sun God Michael! Wow!"
"Wow!", I repeated. It had sure been some evening.
"Wow", said Cleopatra, and she kissed me, saying, "can I have some scotch?"

I went to bed. I couldn't sleep but nevertheless went to work at Stockport MBC the next day, although I must admit I did think of ringing in sick. And then after my day at Stockport I went to work again delivering pizzas until 2am. But I'd resolved by then to give it up. Ra was right. It had no point any more. So I have.

I reflect. We have all worked so hard to get this far, to uncover the mystery of God, the Sun God, and Creation. And we have succeeded. We have found a reasonable supreme being at last, the ultimate creator of everything, the Sun God Ra Himself. And Versailles shall be ours. So give it to us.

www.ingramcontent.com/pod-product-compliance
Lightning Source LLC
LaVergne TN
LVHW091007080826
845145LV00003B/1160

* 9 7 8 1 8 4 9 9 1 0 0 4 0 *